FIRST
CENTURY
FOUNDATIONS

JOSEPH F. AMARAL

All Scripture references are taken from the New International Version unless otherwise noted.

Published by:
    Almond Publications
    908 Lancaster Boulevard
    Milton, ON L9T 6A4

Printed in Canada by Pro Impressions

ISBN: 0-921715-04-8

DEDICATION & ACKNOWLEDGEMENTS

There are many people who are responsible for the writing of this book. I want to lovingly acknowledge my wife Karen for standing with me so patiently during this project—this book is dedicated to her. She poured countless hours into the formatting and design of this book. Without her assistance, this book would not exist. I want to thank both our children Katelyn and Daniel for being so understanding with Daddy's travel schedule to make this book happen. I love you all very much.

This book is also dedicated to my Mom and Dad, Maria Jose and Francisco Amaral. I want to thank them for all the sacrifices they've made in their lives for me. Can you believe I wrote a book?

Also to my in-laws, Clyde and Marion Williamson, who have loved me like their own son. They have contributed in so many ways to accomplish this project. Believe me, I appreciate them all.

I want to especially thank the Lord for a very special couple in my life. Their obedience to the Lord and generosity towards me made my first trip to Israel possible. The Lord used that very first trip to open up my eyes to the importance of our Hebraic Roots. Thank You! I am forever changed!

Contents

1. Introduction 3
2. First Century Idioms Explained 5
3. First Century Culture within the Life of Jesus 7
4. The Four Messianic Miracles of Jesus 25
5. The Feasts Introduction 31
6. An Overview of the Early Church and the Feasts 35
7. The Feast of Passover 39
8. The Feast of Unleavened Bread 49
9. The Feast of Firstfruits 53
10. The Feast of Pentecost 61
11. The Feast of Trumpets 67
12. The Day of Atonement 81
13. The Feast of Tabernacles 87

INTRODUCTION

Have you ever wondered who Jesus really was? I mean really wondered who He was as a person who lived and walked on this earth? It's a pretty wild topic when you stop and think about it. Here is the Son of the Living God—alive and dwelling with man. What a thought!

Then comes the question of what was He like? What kinds of things did He do or say? What kind of a person was He? In order to answer some of those questions I believe we have to reprocess the information we have come to accept about Him.

In November of 2002, I had the opportunity to visit the Land of Israel for a couple of weeks. On one of the days we were standing on one of the most famous historical spots. From where we stood you could look down and take a breathtaking view of Jerusalem. It was from this place, or one like it, the Scriptures tell us in Matthew 9:36 that Jesus was moved with compassion for the people of Jerusalem. From that spot as you look to the right you could see the ancient Jewish burial sites and the tombs of some of Israel's greatest kings and Old Testament legends.

As you look to the centre, your eyes behold the Old City of David and the Kidron Valley where Jesus and His disciples walked numerous times. To the far and upper right you can see the Mount of Olives where Jesus will step foot when He returns, and you can see where the Temple used to stand. To the upper left you see the splendor of the Old City of Jerusalem. You stand there mesmerized as you gaze upon its massive walls. It was truly breathtaking. I felt as though I could live in that moment forever.

Then I turned to a friend who was near me and told Him that I had just made a remarkable discovery. By the look on my face and the largeness of my eyes, he knew that whatever it was, it was big. He was wondering about what incredible thought or revelation did I just have that was going to change our lives and our world? I said to him, "Jesus was a Jew," and when I said it I grabbed my own mouth and covered it. I couldn't believe what I had just said. Then he looked at me with the same look of bewilderment I had just had and he said, "Yah! He wasn't from Montana, was He?!"

Only moments later did I realize the full impact that statement had on me. Jesus wasn't from Montana, nor was He a Canadian—He was a Jew living in First Century Israel, living a First Century lifestyle.

That realization has forever impacted the way I see Jesus, and the way in which I now perceive the Gospels. During the rest of the trip in

Israel I kept looking around at people and the land and buildings and it became more and more powerful. This is where Jesus lived and died, where He rose from the dead and it is the land and people to which He will return.

Out of that realization also came a deep desire from within my spirit—I would make it my purpose in this life to discover the historical Jesus who lived and taught in the Land of Israel. What were people like in general during that historical period? What were their thoughts like, what was going on in the then-known world? How was it affecting Israel and what kind of Messiah where they expecting as well?

The pages to follow are a product of just such questions. As I began to ask the questions I also began to seek out some answers. I read a few books; I researched on the internet; I sat under the teaching of a Rabbi and Messianic Jewish believers; and I pleaded with them to tell me who Jesus really was.

As you read the words on the pages in this document may the Spirit of Messiah capture you as He did me. May the God of all wisdom and peace favor you this day.

FIRST CENTURY IDIOMS EXPLAINED

To understand the sayings of Jesus as they were fully intended, it is important to lay a foundation for our thought process. Idioms, in their simplest explanation, are words or phrases that only make sense in a particular geographical location or within a certain period of history.

In order to better understand the power of an idiom it will be to our benefit to examine what we would call a North American idiom—phrases such as "straight from the horse's mouth" or "it's raining cats and dogs." Statements like these in the western part of the world need no explanation. Anyone living in North America would instantly understand the message of such idioms.

Let's take this thought one step further. Imagine going to a land in the Middle East, or into the deep of the African jungle and using these idioms in attempting to communicate to those from that land. What would someone in a remote part of that land think of if, in the middle of a rainstorm, you were to tell them that it was "raining cats and dogs"? Could you imagine the expression on their faces and the sheer anticipation to see either a cat or a dog fall down on them from the heavens? What if their spiritual leaders attempted to assimilate that saying into their culture without fully understanding its intended meaning?

It's a ridiculous argument you say. Are we not guilty of doing the very same thing? We have taken the sayings of Jesus and applied them unilaterally into our doctrines and theology while failing to understand the true meaning of the idiom used by Christ. As we strive to be more like our Messiah, to think and act like Him, then understanding what He actually meant must be our greatest priority.

As we embrace the rich Jewish heritage of Jesus we can then begin to better understand his teachings and methods. Why didn't He ever come right out and say that He was the Messiah? Are you sure He didn't? He used something called the hinting method (also known in Hebrew as the Remez method). This method of teaching was commonly used in the First Century by Rabbis when debating the Torah and when making a point. A rabbi would quote a verse in part and that would immediately draw the minds of the audience to the entire portion of scripture he was referring to. Another method would be to answer a question with a question. For example when the teachers of the law questioned Jesus about whether or not to pay taxes to Caesar, He answered their question with the question of, "Whose image is on the coin?" This, and countless more truths await you as you discover who Yeshua (Jesus) really was.

FIRST CENTURY CULTURE
WITHIN THE LIFE OF JESUS

1. The Tzitzit (Prayer Shawl) Prophecy

The first story we will look at is of the woman with the issue of blood. For our intent it would be best to read the story in its entirety, then we will return to it and address it from a First Century perspective.

Here is the account in Mark 5:25-29—*"And a woman was there who had been subject to bleeding for twelve years. She had suffered a great deal under the care of many doctors and had spent all she had, yet instead of getting better she grew worse. When she heard about Jesus, she came up behind him in the crowd and touched his cloak, because she thought, "If I just touch his clothes, I will be healed." Immediately her bleeding stopped and she felt in her body that she was freed from her suffering."*

This is a well known portion of scripture that has been preached countless times I'm sure. Having pastored for almost ten years myself, I know I have preached on this. It is probable that we have all preached the same thing—that this was a passage about determination; that we need to be like the woman with the issue of blood; press in through the crowds, and don't worry about what other people say; just touch Jesus and you will be healed. For the most part, this is the extent of which the passage is preached, and it's a valid and excellent message.

What is important to note about this passage is that she reached for the hem of His garment. The Greek word for garment here is "kraspedon", meaning "a tassel of twisted wool". So, in fact, she reached for the tassel at the end of His garment. Why is that important? Why does Mark draw our attention to the fact that she reached for and touched the tassel on His garment?

First of all we should identify what it was in fact that Jesus was wearing. It was commanded by God in Numbers 15:37-41—*"The Lord said to Moses, 'Speak to the Israelites and say to them: 'Throughout the generations to come you are to make tassels on the corners of your garments, with a blue cord on each tassel. You will have these tassels to look at and so you will remember all the commands of the Lord, that you may obey them and not prostitute yourselves by going after the lusts of your own hearts and eyes. Then you will remember to obey all my commands and will be consecrated to your God. I am the Lord your God, who brought you out of Egypt to be your God. I am the Lord your God.'"* Again the Lord commanded them in Deuteronomy 22:12—*"Make tassels on the four corners of the cloak you wear."*

Therefore, according to the Scriptures, Jesus was wearing a garment known as a tzitzit which was common for men in First Century Israel. In Numbers 15:38, the word translated for "border" or "corner" is the Hebrew word "kanaph", which can also be translated "wings". Therefore, the corners of the prayer shawl are often called the wings of the garment. Each prayer shawl was made of eight threads and five double knots, which has a total numeric value of thirteen. The Hebraic numerical value for the word "tzitzit" is six hundred. Add these together and you have a total of six hundred and thirteen, which points to the six hundred and thirteen commandments of the law.

During the first century there had risen a belief about the tzitzit concerning the Messiah. One of them was that the tassels of Messiah's garment possessed healing powers. This, no doubt, is linked to Malachi 4:2a (KJV)—*"But unto you that fear my name shall the Sun of righteousness arise with healing in his wings."* So it was believed in Jesus' day that the Messiah would come with healing in His wings, or His tzitzit. The woman with the issue of blood lived in First Century Israel and was aware of this belief. When she heard that Jesus—who was possibly the Messiah—was passing by, it would explain why she aimed for and touched the tassel on His garment.

You know the story: Jesus realizes that power has gone out from Him. He asks His disciples to find out who touched Him. The disciples have no way of knowing because the crowds are pressed up against them, but Jesus insisted on knowing who had touched Him. The woman comes forward and explains her situation to Jesus. She has this issue of blood—she has had it for twelve years. She has spent all her money with doctors only to have it become worse with time. At that point Jesus commends her and attributes her healing to her faith.

She heard that the Messiah was passing through her town, and He was coming with healing in His wings. It was her faith in the fact that Jesus was her long awaited Messiah that healed her. So, in fact, the tassels had nothing to do with her healing, her faith was in the person who was wearing the tassels—the Messiah.

We now follow Jesus as He continues to the other side of Galilee to seek a time of rest. However as we can see from the text below there was no rest waiting for Jesus but rather the opposite as found in Mark 6:53-56—*"When they had crossed over, they landed at Gennesaret and anchored there. As soon as they got out of the boat, people recognized Jesus. They ran throughout that whole region and carried the sick on mats to wherever they heard he was. And wherever he went—into vil-*

lages, towns or countryside—they placed the sick in the marketplaces. They begged him to let them touch even the edge of his cloak, and all who touched him were healed." The word used here for edge is once again "kraspedon"—the Greek word for tassel. Just as the woman with the issue of blood was healed upon touching the tassel of Jesus' garment, all who touched the tassel of His garment were also healed.

2. Binding and Loosing

The subject of binding and loosing is one of the most misunderstood concepts of all the teachings of Jesus. As we begin to study this saying, we will begin by reading the passage in Matthew 16:13-20—"When Jesus came to the region of Caesarea Philippi, he asked his disciples, 'Who do people say the Son of Man is?' They replied, 'Some say John the Baptist; others say Elijah; and still others, Jeremiah or one of the prophets.' 'But what about you?' He asked. 'Who do you say I am?' Simon Peter answered, 'You are the Christ, the Son of the living God.' Jesus replied, 'Blessed are you, Simon son of Jonah, for this was not revealed to you by man, but by my Father in heaven. And I tell you that you are Peter, and on this rock I will build my church, and the gates of Hades will not overcome it. I will give you the keys of the kingdom of heaven; whatever you bind on earth will be bound in heaven, and whatever you loose on earth will be loosed in heaven.' Then he warned his disciples not to tell anyone that he was the Christ."

This is a historic moment in the life of both Jesus and of Peter's. Jesus is recognized as the Messiah by one of His own disciples, and equally powerful is the fact that Peter is the first of the disciples to recognize that Jesus is the Messiah—a great moment for sure.

What did Jesus mean when He told Peter that whatever he bound on earth would be bound in Heaven, and whatever he loosed on Earth would be loosed in Heaven? Since the introduction of this passage to the western world it has long been believed that Jesus was giving Peter authority to bind and loose demonic spirits from people.

However, in First Century Israel, the terms "binding" and "loosing" were legal terms. They were used to make determinations in laws pertaining to unclear commands of the Torah. To "bind" something meant to forbid it, and to "loose" something meant to permit it. For example, the Bible forbids working on the Sabbath but does not give any clear instructions on what would constitute work. So many times the Rabbis were called upon to settle disputes that would have arisen amongst the people to determine what would or what would not be defined as work.

The Rabbis would hear the arguments and then make a decision. If the Rabbi determined that what was being stated was considered work, he would then "bind" or forbid that particular activity from being done on the Sabbath. If he felt the activity was not work then he would "loose" or permit the activity.

Let's take another glance at what Jesus said to Peter, *"I will give you the keys of the kingdom of heaven; whatever you bind on earth will be bound in heaven, and whatever you loose on earth will be loosed in heaven"*. In the light of what that statement meant in First Century Israel, Jesus was giving Peter the authority to make rulings over spiritual matters within the early Church.

Basically, Jesus was saying that whatever Peter would decide would be backed or approved or accepted by Heaven. What an awesome responsibility! We see in the book of Acts a clear example of Peter's authority to bind and loose. Acts 15:5-20—*"Then some of the believers who belonged to the party of the Pharisees stood up and said, 'The Gentiles must be circumcised and required to obey the law of Moses.' The apostles and elders met to consider this question. After much discussion, Peter got up and addressed them: 'Brothers, you know that some time ago God made a choice among you that the Gentiles might hear from my lips the message of the gospel and believe. God, who knows the heart, showed that he accepted them by giving the Holy Spirit to them, just as he did to us. He made no distinction between us and them, for he purified their hearts by faith. Now then, why do you try to test God by putting on the necks of the disciples a yoke that neither we nor our fathers have been able to bear? No! We believe it is through the grace of our Lord Jesus that we are saved, just as they are.' The whole assembly became silent as they listened to Barnabas and Paul telling about the miraculous signs and wonders God had done among the Gentiles through them.*

"When they finished, James spoke up: 'Brothers, listen to me. Simon has described to us how God at first showed his concern by taking from the Gentiles a people for himself. The words of the prophets are in agreement with this, as it is written: 'After this I will return and rebuild David's fallen tent. Its ruins I will rebuild, and I will restore it, that the remnant of men may seek the Lord, and all the Gentiles who bear my name, says the Lord, who does these things' that have been known for ages. It is my judgment, therefore, that we should not make it difficult for the Gentiles who are turning to God. Instead we should write to them, telling them to abstain from food polluted by idols, from sexual immorality, from the meat of strangled animals and from blood.'"

Peter "loosed" the Gentiles from having to be circumcised and the requirements of the Law. And James gave an example of "binding" when he stated four elements of Pagan practices that the Gentiles were required to abstain from. Having been introduced to the First Century meaning of these two terms, how does it or should it affect Church life today? I believe there is a significant implication for the Church today. Peter was the newly appointed leader of the recently birthed Church and Jesus had given him full authority to make decisions on spiritual matters regarding the Church. In order for the Church to function as God intended it to function, then we need to get back to the Biblical blueprints of the authority structure Christ laid out for us to follow.

3. The True Vine

The statement, "I am the true vine," is a familiar one to us, as the Lord used it several times in the Gospels. What did He actually mean when He said this? What implications were there that people living in that day would have understood it to mean?

John 15:1-8—*"I am the true vine, and my Father is the gardener. He cuts off every branch in me that bears no fruit, while every branch that does bear fruit he prunes so that it will be even more fruitful. You are already clean because of the word I have spoken to you. Remain in me, and I will remain in you. No branch can bear fruit by itself; it must remain in the vine. Neither can you bear fruit unless you remain in me. I am the vine; you are the branches. If a man remains in me and I in him, he will bear much fruit; apart from me you can do nothing. If anyone does not remain in me, he is like a branch that is thrown away and withers; such branches are picked up, thrown into the fire and burned. If you remain in me and my words remain in you, ask whatever you wish, and it will be given you. This is to my Father's glory, that you bear much fruit, showing yourselves to be my disciples."*

During the time of Jesus, which was known as the Second Temple era, a beautiful golden vine was draped across the four pillars to the entrance of the temple. Its beauty was so great that it held great significance in the heart of all who saw it. During that period in temple history many people would make free will offerings of gold and precious metals to add to the vine. Those who gave large amounts often had their name engraved on golden leaves for all to see.

When Jesus spoke of Himself as the "True Vine" he was undoubtedly comparing Himself to this golden vine on the temple. What He was saying to His disciples was that they should invest in Him who was the true and living vine of God, and if they did so they would not yield artificial fruit but eternal fruit.

4. Peter's Use of the Sword

John 18:10—*"Then Simon Peter, who had a sword, drew it and struck the high priest's servant, cutting off his right ear."*

Peter didn't strike the ear of just anyone that day in the garden, but again the Scriptures are careful to tell us that it was the assistant to the high priest who had his ear cut off. His position in Hebrew is known as the "segan hacohaneem". It has been the position of many in the Western Church that it was Peter's intention to cut off his head, but missed.

It is highly unlikely that Peter would miss from two or three feet away from the person. In fact, Peter did exactly what he intended to do. According to Judaic law it would have shamed and disqualified the servant for service in the temple. Consider what the Bible says in Leviticus 21:16-23—*"The Lord said to Moses, 'Say to Aaron: 'For the generations to come none of your descendants who has a defect may come near to offer the food of his God. No man who has any defect may come near: no man who is blind or lame, disfigured or deformed; no man with a crippled foot or hand, or who is hunchbacked or dwarfed, or who has any eye defect, or who has festering or running sores or damaged testicles. No descendant of Aaron the priest who has any defect is to come near to present the offerings made to the Lord by fire. He has a defect; he must not come near to offer the food of his God. He may eat the most holy food of his God, as well as the holy food; yet because of his defect, he must not go near the curtain or approach the altar, and so desecrate my sanctuary. I am the Lord, who makes them holy.'"*

If a person had any of the defects as mentioned in the above passage then he was disqualified from ever working in the temple again. This was not the first time nor the last time this had been done. The historian Josephus of the Second Temple period records several of such like disqualifications.

5. Let the Dead Bury the Dead

Matthew 8:21-22—*"Another disciple said to him, 'Lord, first let me go and bury my father.' But Jesus told him, 'Follow me, and let the dead bury their own dead.'"*

Without proper understanding of cultural practices during the time of Jesus, the above statement of Jesus can sound very harsh, and it would seem that Jesus is telling this disciple to break the fifth commandment found in Exodus 20:12—*"Honour your father and your mother, so that you may live long in the land the Lord your God is giving you."* His remarks were aimed at a Jewish burial tradition that violated the Scripture.

Do you really think that Jesus, being the very form of God Himself would tell a disciple to desecrate the very commandment He gave? I don't think so. In order to fully understand the real meaning behind the seemingly harsh remark, one must understand the burial practices that were observed by those living in First Century Israel.

This tradition required that the body of the deceased be buried the same day. We can see this in Deuteronomy 21:22-23—*"If a man guilty of a capital offense is put to death and his body is hung on a tree, you must not leave his body on the tree overnight. Be sure to bury him that same day, because anyone who is hung on a tree is under God's curse. You must not desecrate the land the Lord your God is giving you as an inheritance."*

Another passage that shows us this can be found in Acts 5:6-10—*"Then the young men came forward, wrapped up his body, and carried him out and buried him. About three hours later his wife came in, not knowing what had happened. Peter asked her, 'Tell me, is this the price you and Ananias got for the land?' 'Yes,' she said, 'that is the price.' Peter said to her, 'How could you agree to test the Spirit of the Lord? Look! The feet of the men who buried your husband are at the door, and they will carry you out also.' At that moment she fell down at his feet and died. Then the young men came in and, finding her dead, carried her out and buried her beside her husband."*

You will notice in both of these passages that the body was buried the same day. This was called the "first burial". After this, the family then was to observe a seven day period of mourning called "shivah". During this special mourning period they were not even permitted to leave the house.

The body was then placed in a burial chamber where it was left to decompose. The Jerusalem Talmud says, "When the flesh had wasted away, the bones were collected and placed in small chests called ossuaries. After the flesh had gone from the bones, and the bones were placed in the ossuaries, the son stopped mourning."

The transfer of the bones to the ossuary was known as what was called the "second burial". What would happen is that the oldest son would take the bones of his father and either take it to the Holy City of Jerusalem or it was taken to the family burial cave where it was to be laid by the bones of their ancestors. Although it did not have a Scriptural basis, this had become a popular practice during the time of Jesus. This was a practice Jesus did not approve of because it was given by man and not by God.

The belief in First Century Israel was that during the decomposing of the flesh from the bones between the first and second burial, atonement for the person was achieved. It was only after the sinful flesh was off the bones could the sins be atoned for. So, as we can see, Jesus was in no way hindering the disciple from keeping the fifth commandment. He was opposed to the second burial that was the idea that anything other than the Messiah could deliver a person from sin.

Some have used this passage to suggest that Jesus was saying that ministry comes before family. Some have even gone as far as to say that family must never come before ministry—that it is a sin. In light of what we know about this passage, according to First Century tradition, that type of thinking could not be further from the truth.

6. The Camel and the Eye of the Needle

Matthew 19:24—*"Again I tell you, it is easier for a camel to go through the eye of a needle than for a rich man to enter the kingdom of God."*

This is one of the most commonly misunderstood teachings in the ministry of Jesus. There have been all kinds of theories brought forth to try to explain this seemingly difficult teaching. Like many of the other teachings of Jesus, this one has been severely misunderstood because of our lack of understanding of First Century Culture and their figures of speech.

One of the most common explanations of this text is that there used to be a very low gate in Jerusalem called "the eye of the needle". The teaching was that the camel could not pass through the gate unless it stooped down on all fours and had all its baggage removed first. This makes a great sermon illustration for sure—that in order to come to God, we must first fall to our knees and remove all of our baggage before coming into His presence. Great illustration, but unfortunately it's unfounded.

It is important to state that no such gate has ever been found in any archaeological excavation. Also, you have to think through the theory of a small gate. It just doesn't make any sense. In ancient Israel the camel was one of the main sources of travel for long distance journeys. Because Jerusalem was home to the temple, it was a very transient city, bringing in travelers from all over the world to celebrate the Passover and the other Biblical holidays. Why would anyone who knows full well that camels would be coming in and of the city on a regular basis build a city with such a small gate? To do so would be foolishness.

There are two key words that have to be examined in order to come to the proper interpretation and understanding of this teaching—they are "camel" and "needle". The Greek helps us to understand the needle. The word used in both Matthew and Mark is the word "rafic." In Luke it is the word "belone." Both refer to needles used in sewing. Therefore, the text is not referring to a gate but to an actual needle.

The Greek also sheds some light on the word for camel. It is possible that the wrong word was used in translation because of the similarity of the spelling in the Greek language. The word "kamilos" means camel, while the word "kamelos" means cable or rope. This helps bring clarity to what Jesus was, in fact, teaching. Of even greater help to us in finding the original meaning of the passage is in the Ancient Aramaic word used in the text. We have to remember that Jesus spoke Aramaic and Hebrew, not Greek or Latin. The Ancient Aramaic word is "gamla" and is the same word for both camel and rope. This is possible because the rope referred to was made of camel hair! The rope was made in a very thick braided fashion and was sometimes used to tie down ships that came into port. So you can imagine how thick and strong this rope would have been.

So with this new information we can see we do not have to explain away the meaning of this teaching. In fact it is very clear what Jesus was trying to teach. The text could read something like this then, "Again I tell you, it is easier for a thick braided rope to go through the eye of a needle than for a rich man to enter the kingdom of God."

7. The Writing in the Sand

John 8:3-11—*"The teachers of the law and the Pharisees brought in a woman caught in adultery. They made her stand before the group and said to Jesus, 'Teacher, this woman was caught in the act of adultery. In the Law Moses commanded us to stone such women. Now what do you say?' They were using this question as a trap, in order to have a basis for accusing him. But Jesus bent down and started to write on the ground with his finger.*

"When they kept on questioning him, he straightened up and said to them, 'If any one of you is without sin, let him be the first to throw a stone at her.' Again he stooped down and wrote on the ground. At this, those who heard began to go away one at a time, the older ones first, until only Jesus was left, with the woman still standing there. Jesus straightened up and asked her, 'Woman, where are they? Has no one condemned you?'

'No one, sir,' she said. 'Then neither do I condemn you,' Jesus declared. 'Go now and leave your life of sin.'"

This is a passage of scripture with which we are all familiar and I'm sure we all share one common question surrounding this story: What did Jesus write in the sand? In order to fully understand the events surrounding this story, there are two fundamental questions we need to address—when and where did the story take place?

Let's first address the "where". The text says that the teachers of the Law brought an adulterous woman before Him. This event could only have occurred in one location in the temple area and that would be the Outer Court (also known as the Women's Court and/or the Gentile's Court). This was an area on the Temple Mount where there were no limitations on who could be there.

(Beyond the Outer Court was an area of the Temple known as the Holy Place and in this area only righteous men were permitted to enter there with their sacrifices. Beyond the Holy Place was the Holy of Holies, the sacred chamber where the glory of God dwelled and in this area only the High Priest on one day of the year was granted access. We see a pattern in the layout of the Temple—the closer we want to get to God's presence, the more holiness is required of us.)

Now that we've established the "where", we'll look at the "when" of this event. To pinpoint the day, we need to look back a few hours to what led up to the story we're examining. Prior to this event, John 7:37-44 records that, *"On the last and greatest day of the Feast, Jesus stood (in the temple) and said in a loud voice, 'If anyone is thirsty, let him come to me and drink. Whoever believes in me, as the Scripture has said, streams of living water will flow from within him.' By this he meant the Spirit, whom those who believed in him were later to receive. Up to that time the Spirit had not been given, since Jesus had not yet been glorified.*

"On hearing his words, some of the people said, "Surely this man is the Prophet." Others said, "He is the Christ." Still others asked, "How can the Christ come from Galilee? Does not the Scripture say that the Christ will come from David's family and from Bethlehem, the town where David lived?" Thus the people were divided because of Jesus. Some wanted to seize him, but no one laid a hand on him.'" Some people wanted to accept Jesus as the Messiah and others rejected Him as their Messiah.

John was very specific in mentioning this took place on the last and greatest day of the Feast. The Feast of Tabernacles was known in that time as the greatest feast of Israel and therefore simply became known as "The Feast". As you read through the scriptures, you'll find other feasts are mentioned with their respective names so that is how we know this feast was, in fact, Tabernacles. There was a ceremony associated with the Feast of Tabernacles during the Second Temple era known as the "water libation ceremony." This ceremony took place every day during the feast in the Temple and culminated in a glorious worship service on the last day and that's why that day was known as the "great day" of the feast.

The water libation ceremony was a very involved one. Each day the High Priest would take two empty golden pitchers from the altar area and proceed to the pool of Siloam which was filled with living water (water that has a constant source such as a spring). After filling the pitchers he would then return to the Temple area where he would pour this living water on the altar. This was an outward action of an internal prayer, "Lord, send us Your Living Water." This living water was both physical and spiritual. The physical manifestation was rain.

Israel, being situated in the desert and by nature a very dry place, needs water. The Feast of Tabernacles takes place between mid to late October and is the beginning of the rainy season so this was naturally an appropriate time to pray for the rain that was necessary to life and to a good harvest. The spiritual significance was that God would send His Messiah who would bring the spiritual Living Water to Israel. For many, the daily routine of the sacrificial system had become a very dry practice and they knew the Messiah would bring new life to them.

Imagine being in the Temple on that last day of the Feast and seeing the High Priest pour the living water on the altar in expectation of rain and the arrival of the Messiah. Then a voice rings out from the crowd, *"If anyone is thirsty, let him come to me and drink. Whoever believes in me, as the Scripture has said, streams of living water will flow from within him."* Jesus was boldly and unequivocally stating His Messiahship to Israel. As the text stated, these words of Jesus ignited a sharp disagreement between those who were in the temple area. While some agreed and accepted His claims, the majority rejected these claims. After His rejection by the people He leaves the Holy Place and goes to the Women's/Gentile's Court. So it is after this event our story picks up.

While Jesus is in the Outer Court, the teachers of the Law bring the accused woman to Him for His interpretation of what the Law had to say about her sin. Here we see a prime example of the "Remez method" in action (refer to the chapter "First Century Idioms Explained"). Instead of coming right out and verbalizing His thoughts, He stoops down and writes in the sand. Notice that the accusers take no action at this so Jesus plainly asks for the person without sin to cast the first stone. Jesus is not only addressing the woman's sin but also the sins of the accusatory men. The issue of personal sin is what Jesus is addressing.

There was no response to the first time Jesus wrote in the sand; there was also no response to his direct addressing of their sin but they responded to the second time He wrote in the sand. What was it in His actions that caused the woman's accusers to drop their stones one by one?

Keeping in mind the issue of personal sin and the rejection of Jesus as God's Living Water, we will now focus our attention on a passage from Jeremiah 17:13—*"O Lord, the hope of Israel, all who forsake you will be put to shame. Those who turn away from you will be written in the dust because they have forsaken the Lord, the spring of living water."* WOW—what a passage! Again Jesus is using the Remez method by pointing the people to this portion of scripture. The text says that those who turn away from the Lord (sinners) will have their names written in the dust because they have rejected God's Living Water.

The passage from Jeremiah bears a striking resemblance to the activities as recorded by John. On the greatest day of the Feast—the day the people are expecting God to give them Living Water—Jesus claims to be the Living Water they have been waiting, longing, and searching for. He is then rejected by them and then Jesus writes their names in the dust. It was no surprise the accusers dropped their stones and left. As very well-versed teachers of the Torah, their thoughts would have undoubtedly gone to the passage in Jeremiah and they would have made the logical connection between the prophecy and the actions of Jesus.

8. The Mustard Seed

One of the greatest and most precious of things we, as believers, hold on to is the gift of faith. Faith is the very thing that drives us to continue when our circumstances tell us differently. Faith is what gives us hope to continue against all odds. It is at the core of who we are as followers of Christ. Jesus recognized the importance of having faith and taught His disciples on the matter. In Matthew 17:20 we have a clear teaching from Him on this very matter—*"He replied, 'Because you have so little faith. I tell you the truth, if you have faith as small as a mustard seed, you can say to this mountain, 'Move from here to there' and it will move. Nothing will be impossible for you.'"*

Many of us have read this passage and have been stirred to levels of great faith because of it. Jesus decides to use a mustard seed in His presentation on how to have faith. Why the mustard seed? At this point in our search to find the historical Jesus we must remind ourselves of some very crucial facts about who He was. Jesus was a Rabbi living in the First Century in the nation of Israel. Israel was a nation steeped in religion. What was the religion of choice?—Judaism. So as a Rabbi, Jesus functioned not only in the role of a Rabbi, but also in the methods and practices of one.

One of these noticeable methods is what I would refer to as "the walking and talking" method. Rabbis would journey together with their followers for days at a time while crossing the country—through the hillside, villages and cities. His students or "disciples" would ask him questions. Rabbis being quick on their feet would immediately find something around them that would serve as an illustration from their natural environment. So this brings up our present discussion regarding Jesus using the mustard seed as an illustration. Context is everything and this story is no exception. The story can be found in Matthew 17:14-20.

Matthew 17:20—*"He replied, 'Because you have so little faith. I tell you the truth, if you have faith as small as a mustard seed, you can say to this mountain, `Move from here to there' and it will move. Nothing will be impossible for you.'"*

Matthew 17:20 (AMP)—*"He said to them, Because of the littleness of your faith [that is, your lack of firmly relying trust]. For truly I say to you, if you have faith [that is living] like a grain of mustard seed, you can say to this mountain, Move from here to yonder place, and it will move; and nothing will be impossible to you."*

Notice the subtle changes between the two versions. The New International Version says that we are to have faith the "size" of a mustard seed. The Amplified Version (which takes into consideration Aramaic—the spoken language at the time of Christ) states that we are to have faith that is "living" like a grain of mustard seed. There are two things that we will examine here: 1. What mountain was Jesus referring to here in context to the Jewish world around Him? 2. Why should we have faith that is living like a grain of mustard seed?

The first thing we need to understand about this passage is that the word or term "mountain" used by Jesus was a First Century figure of speech. A "mountain" at that time and within that culture represented a person or thing which held a position of authority. Because of the authority a Rabbi held within a community they were often referred to as "mountains". So when two Rabbis with opposing views would debate on Torah interpretation, the people would often say, "My mountain is going to crush your mountain." An example of this kind of figurative language is recorded by the prophet Ezekiel in chapter 36:1—*"Son of man, proph-*

esy to the mountains of Israel and say, 'O mountains of Israel, hear the word of the Lord.'" Here, we clearly see that the prophet was not speaking to the physical mountains of Israel, but rather those who were the rulers and authorities of the land.

The question that needs to be addressed in the Matthew account is, "What mountain is Jesus referring to?" A loving father brings his demonized son to the disciples who fail in their efforts to cast out the demon. The father then goes directly to Jesus to get the job done. In frustration with the His disciples He casts out the demon.

Afterwards, during a private conversation with His disciples, He teaches them that if their faith can live like a mustard seed, then they would be able to move mountains. The mountain in this scenario then becomes blatantly obvious—demonic powers. In a very real and clear way Jesus tells them that with mustard seed like qualities in their faith, they will be able to move these mountains (demonic powers).

The second question then is, "Why the mustard seed—why must our faith live like the mustard seed?" The apparent properties and qualities of this mustard seed are so uniquely important that Jesus likens our faith to it. Among those in the farming community (which were many in the time of Christ) there was an equally shared frustration surrounding the mustard seed. Mustard seeds are part of the weed family and will grow in almost any environment. We should remind ourselves that Jesus is using rabbinical methods. As He looks around he undoubtedly sees mustard plants around Him as He shares this teaching.

Mustard plants are all around Israel, both in Jesus' time and in modern times. In fact, I am writing this portion of the book today from my hotel room in Tiberias, Israel. Just today as I drove down the highway I saw the roadside covered in mustard plants. They were everywhere. It was very surreal to see these plants growing by the highway where there was so much exhaust and rocks and dry land, yet these plants were flourishing. These are definitely very tough plants—possessing a tenacious quality. You can plant mustard seeds in very rocky areas and because a mustard seed is so strong, when it begins to take root and then spring up, it will quite literally push stones and "mountains" out of its way as it grows. It's no surprise that Jesus said that if our faith was living like a mustard seed that we too would move mountains.

How do we apply this teaching of Jesus to our lives today? What mountains do you have in your life that seem to be crushing you? What huge stone sits upon you today and is either crushing you or holding you back from doing what you know God has called you to do? Whatever it is, you can move it today. Whether it is spiritual forces, sickness, finances or anything else, you can move it! Jesus says that these mountains will be removed. So take courage today knowing that there is nothing in this life that can hold you back and keep you from victory. Today, in Jesus name, you can move that mountain!

9. Show Me a Denarius

Luke 20:20-26 (AMP)—*"So they watched [for an opportunity to ensnare] Him, and sent spies who pretended to be upright (honest and sincere), that they might lay hold of something He might say, so as to turn Him over to the control and authority of the governor. They asked Him, 'Teacher, we know that You speak and teach what is right, and that You show no partiality to anyone but teach the way of God honestly and in truth. Is it lawful for us to give tribute to Caesar or not?'*

"But He recognized and understood their cunning and unscrupulousness and said to them, 'Show Me a Denarius (a coin)! Whose image and inscription does it have?' They answered, 'Caesar's.' He said to them, 'Then render to Caesar the things that are Caesar's, and to God the things that are God's.' So they could not in the presence of the people take hold of anything He said to turn it against Him; but marveling at His reply, they were silent."

This is one of those passages you read in the Scripture and get the feeling you should know more about what was going on in the background. Without any background information the passage can lose its intended message. These spies are sent by the religious leadership who want to trap Jesus so they can charge him before the local governor. The question has to do with paying taxes to the Roman authorities. If Jesus agrees to pay taxes to Caesar then the spies would accuse him of being a traitor to Israel because of His support of the Roman occupation. If He says no, then the spies would go to the local authorities and accuse Jesus of teaching the people to disobey Roman law, and therefore have him charged. This seems to be a "lose-lose" situation for Jesus. However, Jesus gives one response and not only gets off the hook, but He silences His accusers. What did He say or do to put them in their place like that?

To answer this question we need some understanding of First Century rabbinical law. Firstly, we must look at the type of coin Jesus asked them for. He was very specific in the kind of coin He asked them for. He asked them to show Him a denarius (which was a Roman-issued coin). The verse implies the men had one of these coins in the pouches they were carrying with them. By the very fact Jesus asked for that specific coin He was showing the people around Him these men were in possession of this coin. This particular coin bore the image of Caesar who reigned over that region.

These spies came to accuse and trap Jesus of breaking the law. The fact of the matter is that it was these very accusers of Jesus who were breaking the law. The fact they were carrying this particular coin was in direct violation of the Torah. This is what the Bible says about carrying images in Deuteronomy 4:15-16—*"You saw no form of any kind the day the Lord spoke to you at Horeb out of the fire. Therefore watch yourselves very carefully, so that you do not become corrupt and make for yourselves an idol, an image of any shape, whether formed like a man or a woman."*

The Scripture is quite clear on the issue of having an image—they were not to have any image. Here, we see how well versed in the Torah Jesus actually was. He employed First Century rabbinical methods. He demonstrates a working knowledge of Torah and in actuality used the Word of His Father as a means of defense.

There is a very powerful lesson for us here in the 21st Century. Let us not be quick to use our own words as a defense, rather let us follow the example of Christ. Even when the Devil himself came to tempt Jesus in the wilderness, Jesus always responded by saying, "It is written…" Let us not rely upon and use our own words when our enemies come against us, because our words will fail and will not stand the test of time. But as we learn to allow the written Word of God to be our defense we know that it will not return void and that it will silence our enemies.

10. The Gates of Hades

Matthew 16:13-18—*"When Jesus came to the region of Caesarea Philippi, he asked his disciples, 'Who do people say the Son of Man is?' They replied, 'Some say John the Baptist; others say Elijah; and still others, Jeremiah or one of the prophets.' 'But what about you?' he asked. 'Who do you say I am,' Simon Peter answered, 'You are the Christ, the Son of the living God.' Jesus replied, 'Blessed are you, Simon son of Jonah, for this was not revealed to you by man, but by my Father in heaven. And I tell you that you are Peter, and on this rock I will build my church, and the gates of Hades will not overcome it.'"*

Having a working knowledge of Israel's geography and its topography is critical in our understanding of many Biblical accounts. The geography in this passage is crucial to the reader. Understanding where Jesus was when He asked His disciples who people said He was is very important and will shed great light into a very much misinterpreted passage of

Scripture. The text clearly states they were at a place called Caesarea Philippi. Today, in modern Israel, this place is known as the region of Banias. Caesarea Philippi is found at the base of Mt. Hermon in the Golan Heights of Israel not far from the borders of Eastern Syria. This, in fact, was the most Northern region of Jesus' earthly ministry.

About 300 years before the time of Jesus, the occupying force in Israel was the Greeks—led by Alexander the Great. Along with everything that comes with a conquering nation also comes their religion. The religion of the Greeks was none other than that of Greek Mythology. This mythology introduced Israel to the idea of polytheism—the belief of many gods. The Greeks also brought with them their views of worship and sacrifice that influenced Israel for a period of 300 years right up until the time of Jesus.

The epicenter of activity for the Greeks and this new religion was at Caesarea Philippi. Here existed a large sanctuary built for the purpose of offering human sacrifices to Pan, the Greek god, who was part man and part goat. The legend of Pan told that he would roam through the forests playing his flute (hence the name "pan flute"). It was said the sound from his flute was so terrible that people would run from the forest in absolute terror and fear. That is why to this day we use the term "panic" to express when someone is acutely afraid.

Not only was the sanctuary for Pan there but also many gates were carved into the rock of Mt. Hermon. There was an altar for Zeus and other various Greek gods as well. These altars were called "The Gates of Hades". This new Greek religion was sweeping the nation of Israel and was prevailing. More and more of the Jewish people were falling into its lure. The Jews who followed this new movement were referred to as the "Hellenistic" Jews.

People of that religion believed that a man who could perform miracles was a god. We can see this clearly in Acts 14:8-13—"*In Lystra there sat a man crippled in his feet, who was lame from birth and had never walked. He listened to Paul as he was speaking. Paul looked directly at him, saw that he had faith to be healed and called out, 'Stand up on your feet!' At that, the man jumped up and began to walk.*

"When the crowd saw what Paul had done, they shouted in the Lycaonian language, 'The gods have come down to us in human form!' Barnabas they called Zeus, and Paul they called Hermes because he was the chief speaker. The priest of Zeus, whose temple was just outside the city, brought bulls and wreaths to the city gates because he and the crowd wanted to offer sacrifices to them." Clearly after seeing Jesus' miracles in

the region the people must have thought He was some kind of god. That is why in the text we find Jesus asking His disciples, *"Who do people say the Son of Man is?"*

In the light of this we can now see why Peter's confession is so striking. We also have new insight into why Jesus said what He did to him. At the very source of this thriving polytheistic center Jesus says that the Gates of Hades would not prevail against the Church. Jesus, in a very powerful and real way, was saying that the polytheism of the Greeks would not prevail against the monotheism of Israel. He was also saying that this new Greek movement would not prevail against His new movement—the Church. Jesus prophesied an end to this Greek movement with Peter's alarming revelation. Jesus wasn't "a god"; He was "The God" of Israel—the Messiah. His words have come to pass. Greek mythology has come and gone in the land of Israel, but Christianity has continued to grow and is the world's largest religion. Praise God that the gates of Hades did not prevail against the Church!

The Four Messianic Miracles of Jesus

Jesus performed so many miracles, but why did the Pharisees react more to some than others?—A valid question to which there is an understandable reason. Sometime, prior to the coming of Jesus, the Rabbis divided miracles into two separate categories—those that anyone could perform if empowered to do so and those reserved only for the Messiah.

Basically, what happened was that any of the miracles the Rabbis or the Pharisees could not do, they would simply tell the people only the Messiah would be able to do them one day. There has been a lot of speculation in the Church as to why the Pharisees were continually showing up every time Jesus did a miracle.

We have to remember that Israel was desperately waiting for the Messiah. They had been under the rule of an oppressor basically from their inception as a nation. If it wasn't the Egyptians it was the Babylonians, and if not them then it was the Romans. They were tired of being ruled by others and they were waiting and longing for their promised Messiah to set them free.

We need to dwell inside the mind of a person living in First Century Israel in order to understand what they were going through as a people. They were expecting a leader who would lead them in an uprise against the Romans—a man who would pave the way for war. In their desperation for freedom, they forgot what the real purpose of the Messiah was—to bring salvation to all Israel.

Every time there was a possible candidate to be the Messiah, it was standard procedure to dispatch a group of Pharisees to interview and spy out the person. They even went to John the Baptist because the people were saying that He was the prophet that Moses said God would send.

History does record that some of the Messianic miracles were performed by some. So every time a Messianic miracle was accomplished, the Pharisees immediately went to investigate it and thinking amongst themselves, "Maybe this one will be Him! Maybe He will be the Messiah!" You can rest assured that every time someone performed a Messianic miracle that there was a great anticipation in their hearts as they went out to investigate the possibility.

Invariably they would be disappointed, because that candidate would only perform one of the four necessary miracles to be the Messiah. Then Jesus of Nazareth appears on the scene. He didn't just perform one Messianic miracle, nor two nor three, but He performed all four!—Leading them to either conclude that He was the Messiah, or because of jealousy, they would have to kill Him in order to prevent the people from following Him and abandoning their religious way of life.

In this chapter we will examine all four Messianic miracles and we will see that Jesus of Nazareth was their Messiah then, and He's still our Messiah today!

1. The Healing of the Leper

The first Messianic miracle of Jesus was the healing of a leper. Leprosy was considered a curse from God because of sin in your life or sin in the life of your parents. The Law stated that a person would be defiled by touching a leper. You would also be ceremonially unclean or defiled by touching a dead human body, a dead animal, or a live, unclean animal, such as swine. Lepers were considered to be unclean and people could not come in contact with those who were afflicted. Lepers were required to stand down wind and if they were coming near anyone they had to shout out, "Unclean, unclean, unclean".

It's important to note that there were two peopled healed of leprosy, Miriam—who's leprosy was given by God Himself as punishment (Numbers 12:1-15)—and Naaman—who was a Gentile from the Kingdom of Aram (2 Kings 5:1-13).

Only God could forgive sin and therefore only God could heal a person of leprosy and thus the belief was that because only God could do this, that one day the Messiah would come and do this very miracle. In the following passage we find an example of this first Messianic miracle. Mark 1:40-45—*"A man with leprosy came to him and begged him on his knees, 'If you are willing, you can make me clean.' Filled with compassion, Jesus reached out his hand and touched the man. 'I am willing,' he said. 'Be clean!' Immediately the leprosy left him and he was cured. Jesus sent him away at once with a strong warning: 'See that you don't tell this to anyone. But go, show yourself to the priest and offer the sacrifices that Moses commanded for your cleansing, as a testimony to them.' Instead he went out and began to talk freely, spreading the news. As a result, Jesus could no longer enter a town openly but stayed outside in lonely places. Yet the people still came to him from everywhere."*

2. The Casting Out of a Mute Demon

Matthew 12:22-23—*"Then they brought him a demon-possessed man who was blind and mute, and Jesus healed him, so that he could both talk and see. All the people were astonished and said, 'Could this be the Son of David?'"*

It's interesting to note that right after this miracle the people began to ask, "Could this be the Son of David?" or in other words, "Could this be the Messiah?" Jesus performed many miracles, so why did this one place Him as a candidate for the position of Messiah? The answer is because that it was, in fact, a Messianic miracle, and all who were there— Pharisees included—knew it was.

In First Century Israel the Rabbis would cast out demons with a particular method. The person who was demon possessed would be brought in before them. The Rabbis would then ask the name of the demon and then cast it out by that name. But the problem was that when a mute demon was presented, their method could not work because the mute demon could not speak and so the Rabbis could not cast it out. So it was said and taught that only the Messiah would have the authority to cast out a mute spirit. That is exactly what Jesus did and why the people were whispering amongst themselves.

At this point Jesus had performed two of the four expected Messianic miracles. This miracle was a major turning point in the ministry of Jesus. He wasn't just a good teacher anymore, He was being considered to be the Messiah!

3. The Healing of a Man Born Blind

In the following passage we find the third Messianic miracle of Jesus. John 9:1-7—*"As he went along, he saw a man blind from birth. His disciples asked him, 'Rabbi, who sinned, this man or his parents, that he was born blind?' 'Neither this man nor his parents sinned,' said Jesus, 'but this happened so that the work of God might be displayed in his life.*

"As long as it is day, we must do the work of him who sent me. Night is coming, when no one can work. While I am in the world, I am the light of the world.' Having said this, he spit on the ground, made some mud with the saliva, and put it on the man's eyes. 'Go,' he told him, 'wash in the Pool of Siloam.' So the man went and washed, and came home seeing."

This, again, is another powerful Messianic miracle of Jesus. Others who came before Jesus made a lot of claims and said a lot of things, but Jesus backed up His claims with actions. In this passage He tells his disciples He is the Light of the world, and then He proves it by healing a man born blind.

It was taught during the days of Jesus that only the Messiah would be able to heal a man who was blind from birth. Blindness was said to be a curse from God, and therefore only God could remove that curse. The

Messiah had divine status and was equated to being God. So when Jesus performed this miracle it definitely got the attention of the people—especially the Pharisees.

The blind man then begins walking around town and people recognize him as the man born blind. They demand to know who healed him because it was the Sabbath. After hearing it was Jesus they decided to take the man before the Pharisees. They interrogate him and he tells them again, plainly, it was Jesus who healed him.

The Pharisees object and then take it one step further and they suggest that he has been lying about being born blind, so they call for his parents to verify the information. His parents arrive and the Pharisees question them. They confirm to the Pharisees this is, in fact, their son and he was born blind.

After hearing all this evidence they ask the man again to tell them who healed him and how. In frustration he suggests that perhaps they are asking him again because they want to become disciples of Jesus. The Pharisees quickly respond by saying that they are followers of Moses, because he was a righteous man. The formerly blind man then argues that if Jesus was a sinner, then how could God use such a man? He, then, puts the icing on the cake; consider what he says in John 9:32—*"Nobody has ever heard of opening the eyes of a man born blind."* We now have three Messianic miracles; only one more left to complete.

4. The Raising of a Dead Man on the Fourth Day

This is the fourth and final Messianic miracle we will look at. It is so powerful when you understand the Hebraic significance of the passage. Let's take a look at the Scripture in John 11:1-44—*"Now a man named Lazarus was sick. He was from Bethany, the village of Mary and her sister Martha. This Mary, whose brother Lazarus now lay sick, was the same one who poured perfume on the Lord and wiped his feet with her hair. So the sisters sent word to Jesus, 'Lord, the one you love is sick.' When he heard this, Jesus said, 'This sickness will not end in death. No, it is for God's glory so that God's Son may be glorified through it.'*

"Jesus loved Martha and her sister and Lazarus. Yet when he heard that Lazarus was sick, he stayed where he was two more days. Then he said to his disciples, 'Let us go back to Judea.' 'But Rabbi,' they said, 'a short while ago the Jews tried to stone you, and yet you are going back there?' Jesus answered, 'Are there not twelve hours of daylight? A man who walks by day will not stumble, for he sees by this world's light. It is when he walks by night that he stumbles, for he has no light.'

"After he had said this, he went on to tell them, 'Our friend Lazarus has fallen asleep; but I am going there to wake him up.' His disciples replied, 'Lord, if he sleeps, he will get better.' Jesus had been speaking of his death, but his disciples thought he meant natural sleep. So then he told them plainly, 'Lazarus is dead, and for your sake I am glad I was not there, so that you may believe. But let us go to him.' Then Thomas (called Didymus) said to the rest of the disciples, 'Let us also go, that we may die with him.'

"On his arrival, Jesus found that Lazarus had already been in the tomb for four days. Bethany was less than two miles from Jerusalem, and many Jews had come to Martha and Mary to comfort them in the loss of their brother. When Martha heard that Jesus was coming, she went out to meet him, but Mary stayed at home.

"'Lord,' Martha said to Jesus, 'if you had been here, my brother would not have died. But I know that even now God will give you whatever you ask.' Jesus said to her, 'Your brother will rise again.' Martha answered, 'I know he will rise again in the resurrection at the last day.' Jesus said to her, 'I am the resurrection and the life. He who believes in me will live, even though he dies; and whoever lives and believes in me will never die. Do you believe this?' 'Yes, Lord,' she told him, 'I believe that you are the Christ, the Son of God, who was to come into the world.' And after she had said this, she went back and called her sister Mary aside. 'The Teacher is here,' she said, 'and is asking for you.' When Mary heard this, she got up quickly and went to him.

"Now Jesus had not yet entered the village, but was still at the place where Martha had met him. When the Jews who had been with Mary in the house, comforting her, noticed how quickly she got up and went out, they followed her, supposing she was going to the tomb to mourn there. When Mary reached the place where Jesus was and saw him, she fell at his feet and said, 'Lord, if you had been here, my brother would not have died.' When Jesus saw her weeping, and the Jews who had come along with her also weeping, he was deeply moved in spirit and troubled. 'Where have you laid him?' he asked. 'Come and see, Lord,' they replied. Jesus wept. Then the Jews said, 'See how he loved him!' But some of them said, 'Could not he who opened the eyes of the blind man have kept this man from dying?'

"Jesus, once more deeply moved, came to the tomb. It was a cave with a stone laid across the entrance. 'Take away the stone,' he said. 'But, Lord,' said Martha, the sister of the dead man, 'by this time there is a bad odor, for he has been there four days.' Then Jesus said, 'Did I not tell you *that if you believed, you would see the glory of God?' So they took away the stone. Then Jesus looked up and said, 'Father, I thank you that you have heard me. I knew that you always hear me, but I said this for the benefit of the people standing here, that they may believe that you sent me.' When he had said this, Jesus called in a loud voice, 'Lazarus, come out!' The dead man came out, his hands and feet wrapped with strips of linen, and a cloth around his face. Jesus said to them, 'Take off the grave clothes and let him go.'"*

What an incredible story! For many it is a great source of strength to believe God for the impossible. There is also a Hebraic influence in this passage that brings it to life. Rabbis taught that resurrection from the dead was only possible within the first three days. The belief was that the spirit of a person would hover over the body for the first three days after death, and during that time if one was empowered by God to do so, resurrection was possible. But only the Messiah could perform a resurrection on or after the fourth day. With that idea in mind, let's re-think the story of Lazarus. It seemed Jesus went out of His way to be late. It wasn't that He wasn't compassionate or loving—He had a purpose to accomplish. The reaction of the people at the grave is interesting to note.

When Jesus arrived, there was not one person who thought He would do what He did—they all thought He was just being a good friend. Notice what they said: *"Could not he who opened the eyes of the blind man have kept this man from dying?"* That statement was paramount as to the attitude of the people towards Jesus. Basically they were implying by faith that He was the Messiah. "Didn't He do other Messianic miracles already?" was what they were saying. Of course Jesus was fully aware of the beliefs of First Century Israel towards the Messiah. When He asked them to remove the stone, He was declaring His Messiahship in a clear, loud voice and everyone who was there that day knew it.

Imagine the tension and excitement of that moment. Many had made the claim, but here was this man Jesus from Nazareth supporting His claims with miracle after miracle. When Lazarus came out of the tomb alive and well on the fourth day, there was no denying the truth from that moment on—Jesus was the promised Messiah.

That fourth and final miracle was the proverbial nail-in-the-coffin for Jesus. Consider the text that followed Lazarus' resurrection from the dead in John 11:53—*"So from that day on they plotted to take his life."* The Rabbis, the Pharisees and Israel itself could not deny it or question it any longer. They had to either accept Him as Messiah, or do away with Him as quickly as they could. History records their choice.

THE FEASTS INTRODUCTION
Leviticus 23:1-44

For many believers, the first question is always, "Why should we as the Gentile church have anything to do with the Feasts?" Many people often call these the Feasts of Israel or the Jewish Feasts. The bottom line question is, "Whose feasts are they anyways?" To answer this question we need to look at Leviticus 23:1-2—*"The Lord said to Moses, 'Speak to the Israelites and say to them: 'These are my appointed feasts, the appointed feasts of the Lord, which you are to proclaim as sacred assemblies.* God did not call them the Feasts of Israel; He didn't limit them to a people group or to a particular period of time. He said they were His Feasts—His appointed times.

God has a system; He has a strategic way of doing things. In the Feasts we find the revealed nature of God. He gave them to us to help us to understand the way He moves throughout history. The Feasts are not just about Israel and what happened thousands of years ago. They are for us today. They point to the Messiah, both to His First and Second Coming.

The Hebrew word in the above passage that is used for sacred assembly is "miqra" and it literally means "rehearsal". The other Hebrew word used in the above passage for the word feasts is "moed" and it literally means "appointed time". So what is the Lord saying to us about His Feasts? He is saying that they are rehearsals for appointed times.

A clear example of this can be found in the Feast of Passover. The original "lamb" sacrificed at Passover was literally a "rehearsal" to prepare Israel for their true sacrificial "Lamb" who was Christ. The Bible teaches that the Feasts were shadows of things to come. The Apostle Paul says it clearly in Colossians 2:16-17—*"Therefore do not let anyone judge you by what you eat or drink, or with regard to a religious festival, a New Moon celebration or a Sabbath day. These are a shadow of the things that were to come; the reality, however, is found in Christ."*

There are three ways in which you can look at things as they pertain to the Feasts. Consider the following three words: could, should and must. As people who are grafted into spiritual Israel (Romans 11:17) we COULD participate in the celebration of the Biblical Feasts. As we come to understand that the Feasts point the way to the Messiah we can joyfully enter in and make them a part of our lives. As we examine the Scriptures and we see that Jesus faithfully kept the Feasts you might even be prepared to say that we SHOULD keep the Feasts. Where the danger lies is in the final area in where some would say that we MUST keep the Feasts. Like Baptism, it is not a requirement for salvation, but rather it is done out of a natural outflow of our hearts. Every time we celebrate the Feasts we are preparing ourselves for the prophetic fulfillment of them.

They not only point to the Messiah, they are actually fulfilled in Him. As believers in Christ there is so much for us to glean from the Feasts. There are basically four aspects to the Feasts that we will cover in this book. What was the nature of the Feasts? What did the Feasts tell the people about the Messiah? As the Messiah, how did Jesus fulfill them? And finally, what do the Feasts say to us as the church today?

The church has been crying out to God for many years for revival. Many revivals have come and gone. Some have brought much fruit and great results to the body of Christ. One of the key elements to revival is in understanding our Hebraic roots. We have to get back to seeing and worshipping God as the First Century believers did. How did they see God and how did they worship Him?

I believe that New Testament patterns and practices will bring New Testament results. Everyone wants the book of Acts outpouring and the key to the Day of Pentecost's explosive events is in understanding the Feast of Pentecost. How did three thousand men come to accept Jesus as the Messiah that day? Why were they there? How was it that these men who only a few weeks before rejected Jesus were now ready to confess Him as Saviour? Well, we better not jump ahead just yet. We will cover that Feast in great detail in the chapters that lie ahead.

The Scriptures are replete with examples of Jesus keeping the Feasts. We know that He celebrated the Passover with His disciples every year (Matthew 26:18). He attended the Feast of Unleavened Bread (Mark 14:12). He made His most major Messianic claims during the Feasts of Tabernacles (John 7:37). Nowhere in all of Scripture are we told to stop celebrating the Feasts. In fact the opposite is true. The Apostle Paul told the Gentile believers in the early Church to keep the Feasts (1 Corinthians 5:7-8). If Jesus kept the Feasts and Paul tells us as Gentiles to observe them why don't we keep and celebrate them today? I think this is a valid question.

The Feasts were God's way of teaching His people about Himself. If they are God's teaching methods for us then why are we not using His methods? How can we understand God and His plans by using our natural minds and by using our own plans? In order to better comprehend the things of God, the Western church needs to go through a radical transformation in these last days.

The Feasts show us and remind us of God's supernatural intervention in the lives of His people. Every time we celebrate them we are reminded of God's activity within humanity. They are a way of instructing our children. When they ask why we celebrate the Feasts we then implement God's pattern for education. The Feasts show us God's design for salvation. They are the building blocks that contain within themselves the blueprints to helping us identify His Messiah—His Son—Jesus of Nazareth. The Feasts can be described as God's prophetic calendar. They tell us of events past and of events to come.

Many of God's people fall into one of two categories when it comes to feelings about the end times. They are either in the confused category or the fearful group and God's desire has never been for His children to live in fear and confusion. As we begin to examine and understand the prophetic nature of the Feasts something wonderful begins to happen. Confusion is replaced with clarity and fear melts away in the presence of total joy. The Rapture can become an exciting, joyous time, not a fearful dooming event waiting there to condemn us. As you begin to understand your position as His Bride, the Rapture, Second Coming and the Millennial Reign take on an entirely new light.

The Spring Holidays—Passover, Unleavened Bread, Firstfruits and Pentecost—all point to events concerning the first coming of Jesus. The Fall Holidays—Trumpets, Day of Atonement and Tabernacles—all point to events surrounding the second coming of Jesus. It's important for us to note that Jesus fulfilled the first four Feasts during His first coming on their respective days. He didn't fulfill them around the days but He fulfilled them on their actual historical days. If He fulfilled the first four in their actual days, then I would suggest it is reasonable to presume He will fulfill the last three on their actual days. Jesus said we would not know the day or the hour but we would know the seasons. As we understand the Feasts from a First Century perspective and as we celebrate them from a Hebrew cultural point of view, Eschatology takes on a very exciting and interesting dimension.

Those who stand in opposition of celebrating the Feasts today argue that in Christ we are saved and we no longer need to observe such ancient cultural rituals. Celebrating the Feasts should not be done to replace salvation. That was never God's intent for the Feasts. He gave them as a vehicle for humanity to find salvation in His Messiah. We don't celebrate the Feasts to impress God or to try to win His favour. We celebrate them because it reminds us of what He has done for us and what He is going to do. They are like memorials or anniversaries. They are annual reminders of great events. And every time they are celebrated they bring us back to that place of awe, they cause us to see the awesomeness of our great God and King.

The Feasts are pictures for us. Just like in the natural, when we get out an old photo album and we begin to reminisce about former events, we can't help but smile and sometimes laugh when we look at things we used to wear, hair styles of days past. We see how kids and grownups have changed. So too, when we celebrate the Feasts, we smile and are filled once again with worship for Almighty God when we look back and remember the days in which God stepped down out of heaven into our world and forever changed humanity. The more we understand the Feasts, the better we understand God.

AN OVERVIEW OF
THE EARLY CHURCH AND THE FEASTS

At some point in time there came a separation between the early believers and their Jewish roots. After all, Jesus was a Jewish Rabbi who grew up in a Jewish home. As far as the Scriptures tell us He kept all the requirements of the Torah—written and oral. We know that He celebrated the Feasts annually and so did His earthly parents. His disciples kept them and so did the early Church. It's important to note that the early Church was predominantly made up of Jewish believers. In the book of Acts, when Peter stood up to address the crowd he was speaking to, Jewish men had gathered in Jerusalem to celebrate the Feast of Pentecost. Pentecost was what was called a pilgrim Feast. Every male was required by the Lord to travel three times a year to the temple in Jerusalem to celebrate the Feasts. The three pilgrim Feasts were Passover, Pentecost and Tabernacles. So the temple was filled with tens of thousands of Jewish pilgrims from all over the then-known world.

Let's examine the roots of the early Church. We use the term Church quite normally when we speak of the book of Acts, but the word Church didn't come into use until around 325AD. We really should be referring to them as the early believers. These believers, as we have seen from the pilgrim Feasts, were made up of Jewish men and their families. A group of eleven Jewish men preached a message of a Jewish Messiah to a gathered throng of Jewish men in the holy city of Jerusalem. It's quite clear that Jewish practices and ideas would have clearly influenced these early believers. Just imagine what it must have been like for them.

For thousands of years they have been celebrating these Feasts as a people, always in observance and in obedience to the commands of God. They knew that one day God would fulfill His promises and send them a deliverer—a Messiah. And now they have come to faith in Jesus of Nazareth as their Messiah and all of a sudden all of the symbolisms and imageries fall to the side as they see the fulfillments of the Feasts now in Jesus. What an incredible time to be alive!

On the Day of Pentecost, among the three thousand men who came to faith in the Messiah, we are aware of the fact that there were also Gentiles present who came to faith. Jerusalem was a very transient city. Many people came from Asia Minor, Africa and neighboring countries to celebrate the Feasts. While it was true that the Jewish people primarily made up the group of early believers, they were not exclusive to the faith. We know that there were many Gentile believers now in the Messiah.

Within the confines of the First Century believers we find the Jew and the Gentile worshipping the Lord together through their new found faith in the Messiah Jesus (Ephesians 2:14-18).

As the early believers progressed into the Second Century things began to drastically change. Practices the Jewish people had been keeping for years were now being frowned upon by other believers. By the time the Second Century arrived, the Gentile believers greatly outnumbered the amount of Jewish believers.

As a result of the explosion of the Gentile membership, the early Church began to see the process of what has since been known to be called "de-Judaizing". A great resentment of Jewish culture and Jewish traditions began. Things that were accepted before were no longer accepted, and they were becoming less and less tolerated by the others; and we see where the earliest traces of anti-Semitism began.

The Church became more and more influenced by other cultures. Namely, the Roman and the Greek ways of thinking replaced Jewish or Hebrew mindsets. It arrived at the point that even the Biblical holidays were changed, like Passover observance to what is now known as Easter. In the years to follow, even the Biblical Sabbath was changed to Sunday.

Well into the Third Century, Jewish influence was nearly extinct. There were Jewish believers but their practices and influences were no longer welcome in what came to be known as the Church. Under the rulership of Constantine everything began to change. Things that were once accepted were no longer allowed to continue or to be in existence.

Before Constantine, the Gentile believers in the Jewish Messiah, Jesus, were persecuted and were not well received. After Constantine, Gentile believers were no longer persecuted because Constantine converted to Christianity in 325AD and established it as the official Gentile religion. Many other Pagan religions existed at that time and, as we will see, their influences crept into the early Church.

As the Church progressed, things got better for the Gentile believers but they got progressively worse for the Jewish believing community. Any Jew living in that day who came to believe in Jesus of Nazareth as their Messiah was forced to give up and disassociate themselves from everything Jewish, Judaism itself and all other Jewish practices.

Laws were passed that forbade the Jewish believers in Jesus from keeping the Biblical Sabbath. They were forbidden to circumcise their children and they were even forbidden from keep the Biblical holidays such as Passover. Punishment for Jews who were reverting to Jewish practices included imprisonment and even death. So because Constantine banned the Biblical holidays he replaced them with Pagan holidays from other religions.

As we can see from this very brief overview, the Feasts were rejected and stopped by man, not God. The mistake that has been made is in saying that because Jesus already fulfilled the Feasts that they are no longer valid or required of us to remember. That kind of reasoning just doesn't make sense. Just because something has already happened does not make it of any less value or importance. Celebrating the Feasts can bring us encouragement and peace, knowing that Jesus did what He said he would do. And because He fulfilled the requirements and the prophecies of His first coming, we know that He will fulfill and do all that is required of Him at His second coming.

Remember this as we conclude this introduction. It was God who told Moses to instruct Israel to keep the Passover. It was Jesus who told His disciples to celebrate the Passover every year with Him now as its fulfillment. God gave the holidays, and only God has the right to take them away. Many books and articles have been written on the topic of the Feasts. The historical and agricultural background has been researched and represented in an excellent manner by many authors. It is not the objective of this work to reiterate what has already been done. The goal of this project is to bring fresh insight into the prophetic nature of the Feasts as they prophetically parallel the life, death, resurrection and return of the Messiah.

THE FEAST OF PASSOVER

Exodus 12—*"The Lord said to Moses and Aaron in Egypt, 'This month is to be for you the first month, the first month of your year. Tell the whole community of Israel that on the tenth day of this month each man is to take a lamb for his family, one for each household. If any household is too small for a whole lamb, they must share one with their nearest neighbor, having taken into account the number of people there are. You are to determine the amount of lamb needed in accordance with what each person will eat. The animals you choose must be year-old males without defect, and you may take them from the sheep or the goats. Take care of them until the fourteenth day of the month, when all the people of the community of Israel must slaughter them at twilight.*

"Then they are to take some of the blood and put it on the sides and tops of the doorframes of the houses where they eat the lambs. That same night they are to eat the meat roasted over the fire, along with bitter herbs, and bread made without yeast. Do not eat the meat raw or cooked in water, but roast it over the fire—head, legs and inner parts. Do not leave any of it till morning; if some is left till morning, you must burn it.

"This is how you are to eat it: with your cloak tucked into your belt, your sandals on your feet and your staff in your hand. Eat it in haste; it is the Lord's Passover. On that same night I will pass through Egypt and strike down every firstborn—both men and animals—and I will bring judgment on all the gods of Egypt. I am the Lord. The blood will be a sign for you on the houses where you are; and when I see the blood, I will pass over you. No destructive plague will touch you when I strike Egypt.

"This is a day you are to commemorate; for the generations to come you shall celebrate it as a festival to the Lord—a lasting ordinance. For seven days you are to eat bread made without yeast. On the first day remove the yeast from your houses, for whoever eats anything with yeast in it from the first day through the seventh must be cut off from Israel. On the first day hold a sacred assembly, and another one on the seventh day. Do no work at all on these days, except to prepare food for everyone to eat—that is all you may do.

"Celebrate the Feast of Unleavened Bread, because it was on this very day that I brought your divisions out of Egypt. Celebrate this day as a lasting ordinance for the generations to come. In the first month you are to eat bread made without yeast, from the evening of the fourteenth day until the evening of the twenty-first day. For seven days no yeast is to be found in your houses. And whoever eats anything with yeast in it must be

---

cut off from the community of Israel, whether he is an alien or native-born. Eat nothing made with yeast. Wherever you live, you must eat unleavened bread.'

"Then Moses summoned all the elders of Israel and said to them, 'Go at once and select the animals for your families and slaughter the Passover lamb. Take a bunch of hyssop, dip it into the blood in the basin and put some of the blood on the top and on both sides of the doorframe. Not one of you shall go out the door of his house until morning. When the Lord goes through the land to strike down the Egyptians, he will see the blood on the top and sides of the doorframe and will pass over that door-way, and he will not permit the destroyer to enter your houses and strike you down.

"Obey these instructions as a lasting ordinance for you and your descendants. When you enter the land that the Lord will give you as he promised, observe this ceremony. And when your children ask you, 'What does this ceremony mean to you?' then tell them, 'It is the Passover sac-rifice to the Lord, who passed over the houses of the Israelites in Egypt and spared our homes when he struck down the Egyptians'.'

"Then the people bowed down and worshiped. The Israelites did just what the Lord commanded Moses and Aaron. At midnight the Lord struck down all the firstborn in Egypt, from the firstborn of Pharaoh, who sat on the throne, to the firstborn of the prisoner, who was in the dungeon, and the firstborn of all the livestock as well.

"Pharaoh and all his officials and all the Egyptians got up during the night, and there was loud wailing in Egypt, for there was not a house without someone dead. During the night Pharaoh summoned Moses and Aaron and said, 'Up! Leave my people, you and the Israelites! Go, wor-ship the Lord as you have requested. Take your flocks and herds, as you have said, and go. And also bless me.'

"The Egyptians urged the people to hurry and leave the country. 'For otherwise,' they said, 'We will all die!' So the people took their dough before the yeast was added, and carried it on their shoulders in kneading troughs wrapped in clothing. The Israelites did as Moses instructed and asked the Egyptians for articles of silver and gold and for clothing. The Lord had made the Egyptians favorably disposed toward the people, and they gave them what they asked for; so they plundered the Egyptians.

"The Israelites journeyed from Rameses to Succoth. There were about six hundred thousand men on foot, besides women and children. Many other people went up with them, as well as large droves of livestock, both flocks and herds. With the dough they had brought from Egypt, they baked *cakes of unleavened bread. The dough was without yeast because they had been driven out of Egypt and did not have time to prepare food for themselves.*

"Now the length of time the Israelite people lived in Egypt was 430 years. At the end of the 430 years, to the very day, all the Lord's divisions left Egypt. Because the Lord kept vigil that night to bring them out of Egypt, on this night all the Israelites are to keep vigil to honor the Lord for the generations to come.

"The Lord said to Moses and Aaron, 'These are the regulations for the Passover: No foreigner is to eat of it. Any slave you have bought may eat of it after you have circumcised him, but a temporary resident and a hired worker may not eat of it. It must be eaten inside one house; take none of the meat outside the house. Do not break any of the bones. The whole community of Israel must celebrate it.

"An alien living among you who wants to celebrate the Lord's Passover must have all the males in his household circumcised; then he may take part like one born in the land. No uncircumcised male may eat of it. The same law applies to the native-born and to the alien living among you.' All the Israelites did just what the Lord had commanded Moses and Aaron. And on that very day the Lord brought the Israelites out of Egypt by their divisions."

This is where it all begins. Passover was the first Feast to be established (the details of the others came later in time). Passover is foundational and cannot and must not be overlooked when it comes to studying the prophetic nature of the Feasts. There are many parallels between the life and death of the Passover lamb and Jesus, God's Passover Lamb.

The name for Passover in Hebrew is "Pesach"; it simply means to "pass over". The name of this Feast is rooted in the manner in which God said He would protect the Israelites from His final and most powerful plague—the killing of the firstborn male of every home. God said He would send an angel of death to every home in the land. All firstborn sons would be killed accept for those whose families applied the blood of the lamb to the doorposts of their home in the manner in which He would prescribe.

At this stage it's important to note that we should always pay attention to the details of the Scriptures both in the Old and the New Testaments. We have to remember the authors were Jewish and were writing to a Jewish audience. Keeping that in mind, let's begin our journey by paralleling the requirements for the Passover lamb and the life of the Messiah, Jesus.

The first thing we will look at is what I call the letter of blood. In Exodus 12:7 God instructed the Israelites to apply the blood to the doors in a very specific manner. He said they were to apply it to the sides and the top of the door. What we don't know is that by applying the blood in that manner we are left with the letter "Chet" in the Hebrew alphabet. It is the seventh letter and carries the meaning "life". It's amazing to see that God would embed this symbol into the very first command He gives in regards to the Passover Feast. When the angel of death came to a house that had the letter of life on it, it had to "Passover" the house. It's powerful to see that death cannot come to where God has placed life.

There is a question that we need to ask ourselves, have we applied the blood to our doorpost? Have we applied the blood over our marriages, our children and those whom we love and care for? Know that as long as you have His life applied, by faith, to the doorposts of your home, the destroyer can not and will not come in. Every time you face an attack or a difficult circumstance, just turn to the life giving blood of the Lamb.

Though the command was given for the lamb to be killed publicly so that the entire assembly could witness it, the blood of the lamb had to be applied personally. There is so much power in that statement. We know that Jesus was the Lamb of God who was slain once for all, so some would say then that we are all saved because He already died—that's universalism. The truth is, just like the lamb's blood had to be applied personally to every home, we too, by faith, must apply the blood of the sacrifice of Jesus to the doors on our hearts.

The next parallel I want to look at is concerning where the lambs for the Feast of Passover came from. All the lambs came from special fields in the town of Bethlehem, just five miles south of Jerusalem. Contained within these fields were the pure and spotless lambs. Having this picture in our minds, it causes one to stop and wonder if it was the shepherds of these special fields to which the angels appeared and made their Messianic proclaimation when Jesus was born.

Bethlehem consists of two Hebrew words—beit and lehem—which literally means "house of bread". On several occasions, Jesus told the people He was the Bread of Life which had come down from heaven. What more appropriate town for Jesus—the Bread of Life—to be born in than Bethlehem.

Consider also what the prophet Micah said concerning the birth of the Messiah in Micah 5:2—*"But you, Bethlehem Ephrathah, though you are small among the clans of Judah, out of you will come for me one who will be ruler over Israel, whose origins are from of old, from ancient times."*

It was prophesied that the Messiah would come from this little insignificant shepherding village of Bethlehem.

It was the duty and right of the High Priest of Israel to select and declare the Passover lamb for sacrifice. He would go down to Bethlehem to select a pure and spotless lamb. We know Jesus was the Passover Lamb of God, but which High Priest selected Him and where was he presented to Israel as the pure and spotless lamb? John the Baptist performed this role on the day of Jesus' immersion. Luke 1:5 says, *"In the time of Herod king of Judea there was a priest named Zechariah, who belonged to the priestly division of Abijah; his wife Elizabeth was also a descendant of Aaron."*

John's mother was from the line of Aaron, so she is a descendant of the Aaronic Priesthood (the High Priests of Israel). So John the Baptist is from the lineage of the High Priest of Israel and has the right and duty to select the Passover Lamb for sacrifice. Jesus comes to him at the Jordan River and John makes the declaration in John 1:29-31—*"The next day John saw Jesus coming toward him and said, 'Look, the Lamb of God, who takes away the sin of the world! This is the one I meant when I said, 'A man who comes after me has surpassed me because he was before me.' I myself did not know him, but the reason I came baptizing with water was that he might be revealed to Israel.'"* So as a descendant of the High Priest he had the right to declare the lamb for sacrifice, he sees Jesus and he points it out for all to see who were assembled in that place.

John the Baptist was also born at Passover. The time of his birth is of great prophetic significance for us. The Jewish people believed that the prophet Elijah would come before the appearance of the Messiah on earth. This comes from a Messianic prophecy in Malachi 4:5—*"See, I will send you the prophet Elijah before that great and dreadful day of the Lord comes."*

Even today during the Passover Seder or dinner, a special seat and glass is set apart for Elijah. The hope is that he will come on that day. During the dinner a child is sent to open up the front door in hopes that Elijah will come to the door and announce the coming of the Messiah and that he will tell them who He is.

Therefore, John—as the Elijah figure who is born at Passover—declares to Israel who their Messiah is. He chooses Jesus of Nazareth. Jesus affirmed John's role as Elijah in John 11:13-15—*"For all the Prophets and the Law prophesied until John. And if you are willing to accept it, he is the Elijah who was to come. He who has ears let him hear."* So we can see how God was sovereignly working in the background to have all things fulfilled so that there would be no denying His Son as the Messiah sent to save the world from sin.

One of the events of Scripture that has caused me to reflect on is the circumstances surrounding the "Triumphant Entry" of Jesus into Jerusalem. Just think about it for a moment. How was it that on that exact day and during that exact moment when Jesus rode into Jerusalem through the Eastern Gate there was a huge crowd standing there with branches in their hands just waiting to welcome the Messiah? Without proper and full understanding of Ancient Jewish Culture and Temple practices we miss the beauty and power of this momentous day in the ministry and life of Jesus.

Earlier we mentioned that all the lambs for Passover came from Bethlehem. The High Priest would be the one to go down from Jerusalem into Bethlehem and find a perfect lamb. After selecting the lamb he would carry it on his shoulders. The lamb was carried because they couldn't take the risk of the lamb tripping and breaking a leg, because it would no longer be a perfect lamb.

So the High Priest would carry the Passover lamb on his shoulders through the Eastern Gate on the tenth day of the Hebrew month of Nisan—four days before the Passover. Jesus, the Lamb of God, who had been declared and chosen by the High Priest (John the Baptist) is carried on a donkey through the Eastern Gate on the exact same day. As the High Priest would carry the lamb through the town, the people would gather with palm branches and sing praises to the Lord. They would shout, "Hosanna to the lamb of God who has come to take our sins away".

It was a time of great rejoicing because the lamb had been selected. Jesus of Nazareth—who had performed the all of the required Messianic miracles and had met all other required prophecies to be the Messiah— rides in on a donkey on the tail of this very procession of the celebration of the Lamb of God, which is a fulfillment of prophecy. The very fact Jesus rode a donkey is of great prophetic significance as found in Zechariah 9:9—*"Shout, Daughter of Jerusalem! See, your king comes to you, righteous and having salvation, gentle and riding on a donkey, on a colt, the foal of a donkey."*

(Just as a side note ... In ancient times, when a king came into a neighbouring country on a mission of peace, he would come riding a donkey. However, if he came to make war against that nation, then he would come riding a horse. In this simple historical practice, we see another great parallel because Revelations 19:11 tell us, "I saw heaven standing open and there before me was a white horse, whose rider is

called Faithful and True. With justice he judges and makes war." It's awesome to see that the first time Jesus comes to earth, He comes riding a donkey on a mission of peace, yet when He returns to earth the second time, He will be riding a horse to make war against the nations.)

Even the fact that it was the Eastern Gate was important. There are several gates into the city. Why did Jesus ride in through that one in particular? Consider the words of the prophet in Ezekiel 44:1-2—*"Then the man brought me back to the outer gate of the sanctuary, the one facing east, and it was shut. The Lord said to me, 'This gate is to remain shut. It must not be opened; no one may enter through it. It is to remain shut because the Lord, the God of Israel, has entered through it.'"* Ezekiel said one day God would enter Jerusalem through the Eastern Gate of the city, and after that day they were to shut or seal the gate so that no one would be able to enter through it again.

If you have ever been to Jerusalem or have seen a picture of the Eastern Gate today you will find it is completely sealed up and no one may enter through it. In fact, there is a Muslim graveyard in front of it blocking the entrance. So if the gate is sealed up just as the Bible says, then God Himself must have entered through that gate. When did that happen?—The day Jesus entered Jerusalem riding upon the back of a donkey. The gate has been sealed up for all time, until the day the Messiah will come again and walk through its gates.

After the lamb was selected by the High Priest and after it was carried in through the Eastern Gate it was then tied to the entrance of the temple for all to inspect it. They had to make sure that it was without blemish, that it was perfect and faultless. This would continue for four days until the twilight hours leading up to Passover. Jesus came into Jerusalem on the tenth day of Nisan, four days before the Passover. He is then brought into the temple and He is examined or inspected by all for a period of four days. He is examined by the Pharisees and the Sanhedrin. He is seen by Pontius Pilate and then he sent to Herod who found no fault with Him. So he was sent back to Pilate. After four days and after being "tied" to the entrance of the temple, Pilate declared, "I can find no fault with this man." Jesus, the perfect Lamb of God, was declared worthy to be the Passover Lamb.

Another amazing parallel lies in the timing of the sacrificing of the Passover lambs in the temple. The lambs were sacrificed at 3:00 p.m. and Jesus died on the cross at the very same time. It's important to interject at this point that Jesus had no involvement whatsoever in the process of His own death. Some argue that Jesus staged many of His life's events to make Himself fulfill some of the prophecies. Jesus could not have chosen His method of death by crucifixion. He could not have planned for the time of His death to be at 3:00 p.m. We have to accept the fact it was God the Father who organized the order of events surrounding the trial and death of Jesus.

The Passover lamb was to be of the firstborn; Jesus was the firstborn Son of God. We know that the lamb's bones were not to be broken; none of Jesus' bones were broken. The parallels are striking and overwhelming. We can have absolute confidence in the fact that Jesus of Nazareth truly was our Passover Lamb.

Even the place where the crucifixion took place has incredible prophetic significance. Let's look backwards in time to when the Lord spoke to Abraham in Genesis 22:2—*"Then God said, 'Take your son, your only son, Isaac, whom you love, and go to the region of Moriah. Sacrifice him there as a burnt offering on one of the mountains I will tell you about."* Abraham was told to sacrifice his son at Mount Moriah. We are told that because of Abraham's faith, the Lord said He would provide a sacrifice one day. Then suddenly a goat appears in the thicket and Abraham sacrifices it in place of his son. This promise had dual significance. The first lamb was given right away to fulfill the first part of the promise. The Rabbis always saw this promise of a lamb to also be prophetic in nature—that the lamb was a picture of the Messiah who would come to be a sacrifice for them.

I have had the privilege of standing at the place of Jesus' crucifixion in Jerusalem. Some call it Calvary and yet some call it Golgotha—the place of the skull. When you stand there at its base and you stare at the side of the hill, you can see the caves in it which give it the appearance of eye sockets and it truly does look like a skull. What many people are not aware of is that Calvary is actually part of Mount Moriah. So imagine how prophetic Calvary really is.

Thousands of years before the death of Jesus, God promised Israel— through Abraham—that one day He would send them a Lamb for the sacrifice. It was on the very mount where He said He would provide the Lamb—Jesus—that the Passover lamb is sacrificed. The evidence for Jesus is so overwhelming that the truth can no longer be denied. Jesus is the Lamb of God and He truly is the Messiah.

The Bible records an incredible event that took place simultaneously in the temple and on the cross. When Jesus died on the cross something amazing happened in the temple. Let's read from Matthew 27:50-51— *"And when Jesus had cried out again in a loud voice, he gave up his spir-*

it. At that moment the curtain of the temple was torn in two from top to bottom. The earth shook and the rocks split." Why is this important and how does it affect us today? In both biblical and modern times, if a Jewish Father lost his firstborn son he would tear his robe as a sign of grief and mourning. Imagine what was happening in the minds and hearts of those who were celebrating the Passover at the temple.

First of all, we must remember that Passover was a pilgrim Feast—meaning that every Jewish male and his family would be worshipping in Jerusalem. So we know that the Temple would have been overflowing with people and activity. Imagine that as they are worshipping God in the temple, the temple veil—which was protecting and separating them from the Holy of Holies—is torn before their very eyes. The Glory of God is now exposed, they can see into the place where only the High Priest could go. God has just torn His robe because His son has died!

Who is this Son and where is He? They look to the cross and the one who is hanging upon it. They see Jesus who claimed to be the Son of God. They see Jesus who performed miracle after miracle. They see Jesus who has fulfilled prophecy after prophecy in all that He has done. They see Jesus, the Son of God who hangs upon the cross who has become their Passover lamb. And as a sign to all those who are present, which is most likely numbering in the tens of thousands, God tears His robe because He has just lost His son! Wow!

It's noteworthy to mention that Passover is the only Feast which God allowed for the people to celebrate one month later. All other Feasts had to be celebrated on the day which they were given. But Passover offers those who are unable to keep it for whatever reason at a later date. Why would that be? Passover speaks of salvation. Without the shedding of the blood of the Lamb there is no salvation possible. What God, in His mercy, is saying to us is that it is never too late for us to come to salvation. All of our unsaved loved ones still have the opportunity to apply the blood to the doorposts of their hearts. Let us not grow weary in praying for those whom we love to come to salvation. There is still power in the blood. And it is available to all who are searching.

The command from God in the book of Exodus was to kill the lamb publicly so that all could witness its death. But each family had to apply the blood personally to their homes in order for salvation to come to it. If all they did was go to the slaughtering service and observe and then go home without doing anything, surely death would have come to their home that night. They had to observe and then personally apply what had been done for them.

The same holds true for us today. Some people believe in universalism—that all will be saved in the end because Jesus died once for all—but that kind of thinking is foolishness and eternally dangerous. Yes, Jesus died once for all, but just like in the same way the Israelites had to personally apply the blood of the lamb to their homes, so we too must apply the sacrifice of Jesus' blood to the doorposts of out hearts. If, by faith, we will apply His blood to our hearts then we too shall be saved from God's judgment for sin.

As we come to a close of our study on the Passover there is one more area which is of value for us to examine. It concerns the progression of the power of the blood. When Abraham offered up the lamb for Isaac, its blood was powerful enough to cover one man. When the blood of the lamb was spilled on the night of the Passover, its blood was powerful enough to cover an entire family. When the blood of the goats and lambs were spilled on the great Day of Atonement, the blood was powerful enough to cover the sins of an entire nation. But there came One whose blood was more powerful than any that came before. It was the blood of Jesus of Nazareth of whom John the Baptist declared, "Behold the Lamb of God who takes away the sin of the world!" Jesus' blood no longer *covers up* our sin like the blood of all those before Him. His blood *takes away* our sin; He carries our sins away and removes them from us as far as the East is from the West.

THE FEAST OF UNLEAVENED BREAD

Exodus 12:14-20—*"This is a day you are to commemorate; for the generations to come you shall celebrate it as a festival to the Lord—a lasting ordinance. For seven days you are to eat bread made without yeast. On the first day remove the yeast from your houses, for whoever eats anything with yeast in it from the first day through the seventh must be cut off from Israel. On the first day hold a sacred assembly, and another one on the seventh day. Do no work at all on these days, except to prepare food for everyone to eat—that is all you may do. Celebrate the Feast of Unleavened Bread, because it was on this very day that I brought your divisions out of Egypt. Celebrate this day as a lasting ordinance for the generations to come. In the first month you are to eat bread made without yeast, from the evening of the fourteenth day until the evening of the twenty-first day. For seven days no yeast is to be found in your houses. And whoever eats anything with yeast in it must be cut off from the community of Israel, whether he is an alien or native-born. Eat nothing made with yeast. Wherever you live, you must eat unleavened bread."*

This Feast takes place on the fifteenth day of the Hebrew month of Nisan—exactly one day after the Passover—and it lasts for seven days. There are two major Messianic implications regarding this particular Feast. The unleavened bread is a symbol of sinlessness and the significance of the absence of decay in the bread. Let's start by taking a brief look at the origin of the Feast.

This Feast is an annual reminder of how quickly God rescued His people out of Egyptian bondage. Although leaven is a picture of sin and is very much a part of this Feast, I would like for us to consider another characteristic about the leaven and the escape from Egypt. Let's take a look at the passage in context before we examine this topic any further. Exodus 12:31-36—*"During the night Pharaoh summoned Moses and Aaron and said, 'Up! Leave my people, you and the Israelites! Go, worship the Lord as you have requested. Take your flocks and herds, as you have said, and go. And also bless me.' The Egyptians urged the people to hurry and leave the country. 'For otherwise,' they said, 'we will all die!' So the people took their dough before the yeast was added, and carried it on their shoulders in kneading troughs wrapped in clothing. The Israelites did as Moses instructed and asked the Egyptians for articles of silver and gold and for clothing. The Lord had made the Egyptians favorably disposed toward the people, and they gave them what they asked for; so they plundered the Egyptians."*

Verse 34 is of great significance and is often overlooked by many people. The Bible records that God delivered them out of slavery so quickly that they didn't even have time to add the leaven. What a powerful image. The Israelites were in bondage for four hundred and thirty years. Every day it was the same thing; but on this day something happened that was different, something that was unexpected.

Perhaps you can identify with Israel at this point in their journey. Perhaps you have been praying for something for so long that just like the Israelites, you may have stopped believing that it was going to happen. Everyday they cried out to God for a deliverer—to be set free from their oppressors—and God, seemingly, did not reply. When they least expected it, when they were at their end and thought it would never happen, God came through for them. I want you to take courage; I want you to be strengthened. Never give up, never stop believing, because you serve a great and mighty God. You serve the God of Abraham, of Isaac and of Jacob. Keep believing and pressing in. Know that your deliverance is sure and that it is near. As you pray and as you seek, He will deliver you. May your deliverance be as quick as that of the Israelites.

Because God rescued them so quickly they didn't even get the chance to put the leaven in their bread, and as a result of this, their bread did not have a chance to rise. Therefore, God instituted this Feast so all generations would remember how the swift hand of God had moved on behalf of His people. Leaven is forbidden to be in your home during the Feast of Unleavened Bread. Leaven is a picture of sin and therefore must be removed, every trace of it.

The removing of the leaven from the home actually begins one month before the Feast arrives. A tradition has emerged known as the "Bedikat Hametz", or the "Search for Leaven" ceremony. One month before the Passover the mother of the home will go through the entire house and remove every trace of leaven, every bit of bread crumb must be found and thrown out. She will clean every nook and cranny until she is satisfied that all of it is gone. This is where we get what we call "Spring Cleaning".

When it is time for the Feast the mother will leave out ten pieces of leaven throughout the house so that the Father will find it later at the ceremony. The father will walk through the home with a candle, a feather and a wooden spoon. He used the candle as his light to find the leaven. When he finds it he uses the feather to sweep it into the wooden spoon, he then places them in a bag. After all ten pieces are found, the bag is taken outside and burned so that the home is purged from all leaven. This ceremony is done symbolically to show they have kept God's commandment and have removed all sin from their home. It's important to note that you cannot celebrate the Feast while there is still leaven in your home.

The central image or theme for this Feast is the Unleavened or "Matzah" Bread. There is something called the Afikomen that is very important to the application of this Feast. There are three pieces of Matzah bread that are placed inside a Unity bag which has three separate compartments to hold them in. The middle bread is broken during the ceremony and then wrapped in a special cloth and hidden in the home until, a later time in the ceremony, what is called the third cup. People have wondered for centuries why the middle bread is broken and not the top or the bottom ones. Some have suggested that the three breads stand for Abraham, Isaac and Jacob. Some say they represent the Priests the Levites and the Israelites.

The problem with these interpretations is that neither Isaac nor the Levites were broken. So what does it mean to have the middle bread broken? In the manifestation of the God-head we find the answer. We see the Father, the Son and the Holy Spirit. The Son's body is broken, He is then wrapped and put away in the earth and on the third day is brought back to life. So in the ceremony of the Afikomen we find some Messianic fulfillment. This Matzah bread has three certain characteristics to it that set it apart from other types of bread. It is bruised because it is beaten into shape, it has stripes because of the way it is grilled, and finally it is pierced many times to allow for proper cooking.

Within this Unleavened or Matzah bread we find the prophetic fulfillment in Jesus. He was bruised: Isaiah 53:5—*"He was bruised for our iniquities."* He was striped: Isaiah 53:5—*"and with his stripes we are healed."* He was pierced: Zechariah 12:10—*"They will look on me, the one they have pierced."* Another feature about leaven is its ability to permeate dough. Leaven has a contaminating nature. It sours and ferments the dough and causes it to swell it to many times its original size without changing its weight. In fact, this souring process is the first stage of decay. And here we find some more relevance in the death of Jesus.

Psalm 15:10 is considered a Messianic psalm. King David writes *"because you will not abandon me to the grave, nor will you let your Holy One see decay."* Because Jesus was the perfect lamb and the sinless, Unleavened Bread, God did not allow His body to decay. So we see Jesus as the fulfillment of the Unleavened Bread.

So what is God saying to us through this Feast? Is it about not eating bread with leaven it? I think there is something more…profoundly more. Just as the Scripture commanded that the Israelites remove all leaven from their homes, we too are called to remove all the sin from our homes, both literally and spiritually. It was impossible for them to celebrate the Passover with any leaven in their homes. We cannot come into the Kingdom of God with sin in our hearts. We need to ask His Holy Spirit to come and reveal to us any secret or hidden sin in our hearts.

The blood of the Lamb takes away our sin; and the light of the Holy Spirit and of the Word of God keeps us from sin. May we all strive to do what the Apostle Paul told the early Church to do in 1 Corinthians 5:6-8—*"Your boasting is not good. Don't you know that a little yeast works through the whole batch of dough? Get rid of the old yeast that you may be a new batch without yeast—as you really are. For Christ, our Passover lamb, has been sacrificed. Therefore let us keep the Festival, not with the old yeast, the yeast of malice and wickedness, but with bread without yeast, the bread of sincerity and truth."*

THE FEAST OF FIRSTFRUITS

Leviticus 23:9-14—*"The Lord said to Moses, 'Speak to the Israelites and say to them: 'When you enter the land I am going to give you and you reap its harvest, bring to the priest a sheaf of the first grain you harvest. He is to wave the sheaf before the Lord so it will be accepted on your behalf; the priest is to wave it on the day after the Sabbath. On the day you wave the sheaf, you must sacrifice as a burnt offering to the Lord a lamb a year old without defect, together with its grain offering of two-tenths of an ephah of fine flour mixed with oil—an offering made to the Lord by fire, a pleasing aroma—and its drink offering of a quarter of a hin of wine. You must not eat any bread, or roasted or new grain, until the very day you bring this offering to your God. This is to be a lasting ordinance for the generations to come, wherever you live.'"*

The Feast of Firstfruits has virtually disappeared since the days after the destruction of the temple. The principle of this Feast is of first things. Through this Feast we see the Lord speaking to us about two powerful images. The first image we see the Lord speaking to us about is in the area of our tithes and giving to the Lord. And the second picture is in the area of Jesus of Nazareth and His resurrection from the dead as a guarantee of our own resurrection. Before we move into the parallels of this Feast, it would be good for us to lay a foundation and go back in time and look at the original meaning and celebration practices of this Feast.

Like many of Israel's Feasts, Firstfruits operated around the agricultural cycle of the land and time. Barley was the first grain to ripen of all the grains that were sown during the winter months. For the Feast of Firstfruits, a sheaf (about a bushel) of barley would be harvested and brought to the temple as a thanksgiving offering to the Lord for the harvest. The bushel was brought in as a representation of the entire field. The fact they would bring in this small portion was really an act of faith showing God they believed He would bring in a full harvest that year.

The Feast of Firstfruits is the third feast in the Jewish festive cycle. On the Hebrew calendar it occurred on the 16th day of Nisan which coincides with our March or April. As stated in the previous chapters, Passover took place on the 14th and Unleavened Bread on the 15th. Just as these first three feasts happened consecutively, so Jesus fulfilled them in like manner.

It's important to note at this time some of the regulations that were observed by both ancient Israel and the early believers. The people were forbidden from using any part of the harvest until the firstfruits were brought into the temple. Only after their firstfruits were brought into the temple, would they be released to enjoy the benefits of the entire harvest. Reaping from the harvest without bringing in your firstfruits was not only forbidden and looked down upon, but it was being disobedient to a direct command from God. Consider the following scripture found in Leviticus 23:14—*"You must not eat any bread, or roasted or new grain, until the very day you bring this offering to your God. This is to be a lasting ordinance for the generations to come, wherever you live."*

Many modern day believers wrestle with the concept of tithes and offerings. Most people would say that it is an Old Testament model and is not mentioned or reinforced in the New Testament by either Jesus or any of the disciples and that would be a correct statement. The fact is that Jesus and the disciples would not have had to make such a statement because God had already clearly stated His intentions for tithes in the Torah (Law). If we look at the last line of the above verse, we clearly see that God never commanded either Israel or anyone else for that matter, to stop bringing Him our firstfruits. He says it is a statue that is to last forever—to last for all generations and wherever you live.

Notice that God doesn't limit the observance of this Feast to any particular culture, time or place. As a First Century, Torah-observant Rabbi, Jesus knew in His heart—as did every other early believer of that time—that the decree to bring God our firstfruits had not been nullified but in fact the opposite was true. We were to continue, both then and now, to honor God with our firstfruits.

God laid out the framework by which He stated not just how we were to operate but also how He would operate and respond to us. He said if we didn't bring Him our firstfruits that we weren't to expect the harvest. We've clearly seen how God has spoken to us about giving.

Consider the following verse and the severity of God's disappointment when we have failed to observe and obey His statute in Malachi 3:8-12—*"Will a man rob God? Yet you rob me. But you ask, 'How do we rob you?' In tithes and offerings. You are under a curse—the whole nation of you—because you are robbing me. Bring the whole tithe into the storehouse, that there may be food in my house. Test me in this,' says the Lord Almighty, 'and see if I will not throw open the floodgates of heaven and pour out so much blessing that you will not have room enough for it. I will prevent pests from devouring your crops, and the vines in your fields will not cast their fruit,' says the Lord Almighty. 'Then all the nations will call you blessed, for yours will be a delightful land,' says the Lord Almighty."*

It's important for us to realize the reaction that God has to a person who dishonors Him in the area of their tithing. The principle of tithing was not instituted by man, but rather, it was instituted for man. By trusting God enough to bring Him our firstfruits, it's a beautiful display of our faith in God and in His Word. Let us not rob God but let us cheerfully and joyfully follow the instructions of the Lord.

So the people had one part in celebrating the Feast of Firstfruits and the priest also had his role to fulfill. Here we see a very significant role in the person of the High Priest. He does something that is very important for us to realize. There are three offices in the Old testament that were appointed positions by God, and they were that of Prophet, Priest and King. They are known as Messianic types. Basically what that means is that whatever duties they performed or roles they carried out are what the Messiah would also do. We will see how these positions come more and more into play as we continue thought the Feasts. On the Day of Atonement the High Priest would perform very detailed and specific rituals that were pictures of what the Messiah would do on that day. So when we see the High Priest doing something in the Old Testament, you can know that Jesus either performed this duty at His first coming or that He will perform or fulfill it at His second coming. In this feast we are going to see such a role that is Messianic in nature.

According to Leviticus 23:11, the High Priest was to take the firstfruits of the person and wave them before the Lord. God would see this function, He would accept the firstfruits, and then the people were free to enjoy the harvest. Notice the process that's happening here. There are three participants in this Feast—there are the people, there is the High Priest and then there is the Lord. This process could not be completed if any one of these three participants did not do their part. Now we know that Jesus, as our High Priest, will do His part. We know that the Lord, Himself, will do His part. So in order for this process of blessing to work, we must do our part. In just a few moments we will see how the waving of the firstfruits and their acceptance by the Lord is a beautiful and powerful image of what Jesus did at His resurrection.

Although these principles were to be eternally observed by all, this Feast in modern times is no longer observed because of the destruction of the temple by the Romans in 70AD. The Feast of Firstfruits was seen as a marker for Israel. After this feast they would count 49 days (in Hebrew this is referred to as the counting of the Omer) and then on the 50th day, they would celebrate Israel's fourth feast which, Biblically, is called the Feast of Weeks, (hence the counting of seven weeks which equals 49 days) and is known to us today as Pentecost. Only on the 50th day and thereafter would they be permitted to enter into the harvest and enjoy its plenty.

The word that we are going to focus on in Leviticus 23 is the word "wave"His first coming o and it is actually repeated a couple of times. Look at verse 11: *"He is to wave the sheaf before the Lord so it will be accepted on your behalf."* All of Israel was to bring their Firstfruits to the Temple. It's important to note that this is where we get our idea of tithing from. We are to bring our Firstfruits into the house of the Lord. Whenever you came to the temple in scripture, you were to bring an offering before you could enter. We don't bring Him our Firstfruits because He needs them. He's God, everything is already His, but we bring in our tithes as an act of obedience to the Lord. It's good for us to keep this in mind as we continue in our study.

The people would bring in a sheaf of wheat into the temple, then the priest would take the wheat and he would wave it before the Lord. The people would go out into their field and no matter how big it was, they would section off a piece of the crop with red linen before the harvest came into fruition. Note that they marked off the fields before the harvest was visible and not after. They didn't wait to see where the smallest or least amount of harvest was in the field. Because they farmed the same land they knew where the best harvest came from. They would then rope off that section and reserve it as the Firstfruits for God. So then their tithing was pre-meditated and not an afterthought. The people would then take those Firstfruits and bring them to the Temple where the High Priest would then wave them before the Lord. Some feel that the two loaves represented the Jew and the Gentile before the Lord, and through faith in His Messiah, they are accepted into the family of Israel.

Along with the sheaf of wheat they were also required to bring to the Temple with them a loaf of leavened bread. This seems to be a very odd request of the people. In the last Feast there was to be no leaven among them or they would be cut off from the blessing of Israel, but yet during the Feast of Firstfruits God commands them to bring bread with leaven into the Temple. So the question that is begging to be asked then is why must this bread on this day have leaven? The answer is simple but yet so profound.

Like many of the aspects of the Feasts, they are symbolic in nature. Let's think this through as we try to digest the order of events that are unfolding before us. You can't make bread without wheat! Simple but true. The symbolism of the sheaf of wheat and the bread are striking. God is basically saying that by bringing Him the wheat in faith, we believe that He will give us our daily bread. That sounds very familiar. Bringing God the seed was a visible act of faith that God would provide the bread. So if you brought God the seed, He would respond by providing the need. If you did not bring in the wheat, you'd better not be expecting the bread, it's really that simple.

You could not go back to the fields and pick any of or enjoy any of your fruits until your offering was waved by the priest and accepted by God. After and only after you brought your offering to the temple were you permitted by God to enjoy the whole of your harvest. We are starting to see the picture that God has laid out for us in the Feast of Firstfruits? Let's obey God and live under the reign of His blessing!

The Apostle Paul called Jesus our Firstfruits on more than one occasion. What does that mean for us as believers today? What parallels was Paul drawing on and to what was he alluding? These are valid questions. As we begin to dig and develop these thoughts, once again we will find ourselves in awe of what and how God speaks to the Church today through these seven Feasts.

Consider what Paul says in 1 Corinthians 15:20-23—*"But Christ has indeed been raised from the dead, the Firstfruits of those who have fallen asleep. For since death came through a man, the resurrection of the dead comes also through a man. For as in Adam all die, so in Christ all will be made alive. But each in his own turn: Christ, the Firstfruits; then, when he comes, those who belong to him."*

Paul goes back to the fall of Adam and talks about how sin came to all men through him. In like manner, he says that resurrection will come to all believers because of Christ's resurrection. So Jesus is the first to be given resurrection life, and because of His resurrection we are also guaranteed to be raised ourselves. Firstfruits are very important to God, and so now we will look at the duty of Jesus our High priest that we talked about earlier in this chapter.

We established, by Scripture, that the High Priest had to wave the Firstfruits before God in order for them to be accepted. After this process was completed, then the rest of the harvest could be both gathered and enjoyed. Let's see how this is reflected in the resurrection of Jesus and of what benefit it is to us. Consider the following verses as we discuss their implications in Jesus' role as High Priest. Matthew 27:50-53—*"And when Jesus had cried out again in a loud voice, he gave up his spirit. At that moment the curtain of the temple was torn in two from top to bottom. The earth shook and the rocks split. The tombs broke open and the bodies of many holy people who had died were raised to life. They came out of the tombs, and after Jesus' resurrection they went into the holy city and appeared to many people."*

Consider also these following verses as found in Luke 19:36-40—*"As he went along, people spread their cloaks on the road. When he came near the place where the road goes down the Mount of Olives, the whole crowd of disciples began joyfully to praise God in loud voices for all the miracles they had seen: 'Blessed is the king who comes in the name of the Lord!' 'Peace in heaven and glory in the highest!' Some of the Pharisees in the crowd said to Jesus, 'Teacher, rebuke your disciples!' 'I tell you,' he replied, 'if they keep quiet, the stones will cry out.'"*

During the Triumphant Entry, Jesus told the crowd gathered there that He would cause the very stones to cry out if the people were not permitted to freely worship Him. This passage in context is so powerful that it is beyond our comprehension. We have stated over and over again how important it is to understand time and culture. I have been to Jerusalem on more than one occasion, and being there and seeing it with my own eyes has made this verse come to life for me. I now see it in a new light and it has helped me to understand the role of Jesus as our High Priest.

I'm sure many people have the same image conjured up in their mind when Jesus talked about causing the stones to cry out and praise Him. I know what I saw in my mind. I always pictured the stones on the ground standing up and singing the hallelujah chorus or something. I wonder if you share a similar picture. That image has been totally altered in my mind having stood by the Eastern Gate and having seen what is there now and what was all around the entrances to the ancient city.

There were cemeteries all over the sides of the Mount of Olives filled with head stones as grave markers. Please try to get this image in your mind. Jesus wasn't pointing to the pebbles or rocks that lined the streets of Jerusalem. He was referring to the head stones in the cemeteries and was saying that He would cause the dead to rise up and praise Him if the living wouldn't! What makes this discovery more powerful is that Jesus did exactly what He said He would do.

The above text of Matthew 27:52 says that after Jesus died on the cross exactly one week later that the tombs of dead saints were opened up and they were seen by many walking around Jerusalem doing what?— giving praise to God! What happened was exactly what Jesus said would happen. He said that if the living would not praise Him, then the dead would. And they did! I don't know about you, but this brings great comfort to my heart when I think about the power of the words of Jesus. I know that I can have confidence in who He says He is and in what he says He will do. When Jesus speaks and gives a promise we can be assured that it will come to pass. Our Messiah is trustworthy and He is the keeper of His Word.

There were specific duties that were to be performed by the High Priest during Firstfruits. A brief glance into these duties and rituals will bring rich, new insight into the resurrection of Jesus. During the First Century, the common practice was for the High Priest to go into seclusion for three days after the Passover ceremony. After that time he would then go out into a harvest a gather a bundle of wheat from the first grain harvest. He would then present the offering at the temple as the required wave offering. Only after the wave offering had been offered could the High priest come back out into the public and mingle with them. He was not allowed to be touched until after the wave offering had been presented and accepted.

After His crucifixion, which was on the day of Passover, Jesus—our High Priest—went into seclusion (the tomb) for three days. He is met by the women in the garden who want to touch Him, but He warns them not to. We find this scenario in John 20:17—*"Jesus said, 'Do not hold on to me, for I have not yet returned to the Father. Go instead to my brothers and tell them, 'I am returning to my Father and your Father, to my God and your God.'"* Remember that the Priest could only be touched by the people after He went into God's presence and presented the Firstfruits to Him. A few verses later we find that Jesus is encouraging His disciples to touch Him. In the light of this Priestly ritual this is fascinating for us to understand. We find this in John 20:27—*"Then he said to Thomas, 'Put your finger here; see my hands. Reach out your hand and put it into my side. Stop doubting and believe.'"*

After His resurrection He says He is not to be touched until He goes to the Father. A few verses later He is touched by the disciples. That meant at some point between these two events He ascended to the Father and presented His Firstfruits offering. How and when did this happen? When it happened is up for speculation, but we do know how it happened. The saints that were seen walking around Jerusalem were the Firstfruits of the promise of resurrection. They are Jesus the High Priest's wave offering to God. At some point God accepts the offering and Jesus is free to go back to His disciples. And because God accepted those saints as the Firstfruits in Christ, we can also be assured of our resurrection. Jesus our High Priest has fulfilled all the requirements of the Feasts for us. To God be the glory and honor.

THE FEAST OF PENTECOST

Leviticus 23:15-22—*"From the day after the Sabbath, the day you brought the sheaf of the wave offering, count off seven full weeks. Count off fifty days up to the day after the seventh Sabbath, and then present an offering of new grain to the Lord. From wherever you live, bring two loaves made of two-tenths of an ephah of fine flour, baked with yeast, as a wave offering of Firstfruits to the Lord. Present with this bread seven male lambs, each a year old and without defect, one young bull and two rams. They will be a burnt offering to the Lord, together with their grain offerings and drink offerings—an offering made by fire, an aroma pleasing to the Lord. Then sacrifice one male goat for a sin offering and two lambs, each a year old, for a fellowship offering. The priest is to wave the two lambs before the Lord as a wave offering, together with the bread of the Firstfruits. They are a sacred offering to the Lord for the priest. On that same day you are to proclaim a sacred assembly and do no regular work. This is to be a lasting ordinance for the generations to come, wherever you live. When you reap the harvest of your land, do not reap to the very edges of your field or gather the gleanings of your harvest. Leave them for the poor and the alien. I am the Lord your God."*

We now come to the fourth and mostly widely recognized Feast in the Church—Pentecost. The first thing we should note about this Feast is the fact that the day of Pentecost mentioned in Acts chapter two is not the first Feast of Pentecost. Actually, the very first Day of Pentecost happened on the day God gave Moses the Torah at the foot of Mount Sinai almost 3500 years ago. Fifty days after the crossing of the Red Sea—which was a type of Firstfruits—God gives the law to be written in stone. Most believers are under the impression that the day of Pentecost after the resurrection of Christ was the first time it had ever happened in Israel. In fact, as we progress we will see how there was an expectation within the hearts of the First Century people for God to pour out His Spirit on that very day.

Before we proceed any further I think it would be good for us to examine some of the parallels between the Mount Sinai account of the day of Pentecost and the New Testament account of the day of Pentecost. It was during the Feast of the first day of Pentecost that the nation of Israel was born. Before they received the Law they were a wayward people who had just been released from slavery. They knew nothing of being a nation, and were distant from the God of their ancestors. So God birthed the Nation of Israel at the foot of Mount Sinai where His presence was made manifest that day. After such a glorious revelation of God and a historical event of the giving of the Torah, what did Israel do? They couldn't wait for God. The memories of what God had just done was still fresh in their minds, and in the wake of that momentous event they turn away from the God who just rescued them and birthed them as a nation. They turned their hearts away from God and they made themselves a golden calf to worship.

The response that Aaron gave to Moses is classic. Moses left Aaron in charge while he went up to the mountain to receive the law. When he left they were a people who were filled with excitement and anticipation of what God was going to do next. By the time he comes back down they are now worshipping a golden calf. What happened? Aaron says, "We threw in the gold and out came a cow." God's response to this idolatry results in death. So on the first day of Pentecost, 3000 people are killed. Exodus 32:28—*"The Levites did as Moses commanded, and that day about three thousand of the people died."* In this act we see that the letter of the Law brings death.

Now let's turn our attention the day of Pentecost that we are more familiar with—the one after the resurrection of Jesus. At the first Feast of Pentecost the nation of Israel was born, on this Feast of Pentecost the Church was born. Look at the contrast that we find in Acts 2:41—*"Those who accepted his message were baptized, and about three thousand were added to their number that day."* On the day of Pentecost that Jesus fulfilled, it's interesting to note that 3000 are saved. And so in this event we see that the Spirit of the Law brings life.

So then we see the original Feast of Pentecost takes place 50 days after the crossing of the Red Sea. That crossing was a type of Firstfruits, and just like today, Pentecost takes place on the 50th day after the Feast of Firstfruits. Today Pentecost is celebrated as the anniversary of the giving of the Torah, or the Law to Israel. At the first Feast of Pentecost, the Law of God is written on tablets of stone. Remember earlier how we said that the Apostle Paul told us in Colossians that the Feasts were shadows of things to come. So basically what that means is anything that happened during the New Testament or that is going to happen in the future has already happened. There was a shadow, or a type, of it already.

In Acts chapter 2 we read about the great outpouring of the Holy Spirit. We read about this amazing wind and tongues of fire that appeared and fell on everyone, and that all of them were able to speak and understand in different languages. This is a pretty major happening in history. According to the Apostle Paul, this event has already taken place in history. So then the question is not has it happened, but rather when and where did it happen?

Let's examine the events of the first Feast of Pentecost according to rabbinical tradition and then we will compare it to the Acts version and see if we can come up with any similarities. We have the giving of the Torah in Exodus 19. This is where God spoke to the people from Mount Sinai. The power of what happened at this monumental event eludes the English reader. In Exodus 19:19, a trumpet (Shofar) was sounded. The trumpet (Shofar) that was sounded grew louder and louder. Exodus 19:19 says, *"...and God answered him with thunder [by a voice, KJV]."* Exodus 20:18 says, *"And all the people perceived the thunder [saw the thunderings, KJV] ..."* So literally the Bible records that the people who were gathered at the foot of Mount Sinai saw the words as they came forward from the mouth of the Lord.

This is what is says in the Midrash, which is a rabbinical commentary on the Scriptures, in Rabbah 5:9, it says: *"When God gave the Torah on Sinai He displayed untold marvels to Israel with His voice. What happened? God spoke and the voice reverberated throughout the whole world. It says, and all the people witnessed the thunderings."*

It's important for us to note that it says "the thunderings" and not "the thunder". There was a world famous Rabbi by the name of R. Johanan and in this same Midrash he says that "God's voice, as it was uttered split up into seventy voices, in seventy languages, so that all the nations should understand." That's awesome to try and comprehend. So God was not speaking to one particular race or people, the guidelines of the Torah were for all people for all time. Although today there are over 5000 spoken languages know to man, it is widely accepted that all languages can find their roots in the basic 70 languages of the world. The Bible also agrees with this fact. Consider Deuteronomy 32:8—*"When the Most High divided to the nations their inheritance, when He separated the sons of Adam, He set the bounds of the people according to the number of the children of Israel."* In Exodus 1:1-5, it tells us that the number of the children of Israel who came to Egypt was 70. So the 70 voices as interpreted by R. Johanan represented all the nations of the world. So, it was seen that God's voice split up into the languages of all the peoples of the earth to be a witness to them. Wow!

Now read what Rabbi Moshe Weissman wrote in the Midrash about the first Feast of Pentecost, *"In the occasion of the giving of the Torah, the children of Israel not only heard the Lord's voice but actually saw the sound waves as they emerged from the Lord's mouth. They visualized* them as a fiery substance. *Each commandment that left the Lord's mouth traveled around the entire Camp and then to each Jew individually, asking him, "Do you accept upon yourself this Commandment with all the Jewish law pertaining to it?" Every Jew answered "Yes" after each commandment. Finally, the fiery substance which they saw engraved itself on the tablets."* Does that sound familiar to anyone?—wind, fire and different languages being spoken?

Let's look at its counterpart as found in the book of Acts 2:1-11— *"When the day of Pentecost came, they were all together in one place. Suddenly a sound like the blowing of a violent wind came from heaven and filled the whole house where they were sitting. They saw what seemed to be tongues of fire that separated and came to rest on each of them. All of them were filled with the Holy Spirit and began to speak in other tongues as the Spirit enabled them.*

"Now there were staying in Jerusalem God-fearing Jews from every nation under heaven. When they heard this sound, a crowd came together in bewilderment, because each one heard them speaking in his own language. Utterly amazed, they asked: 'Are not all these men who are speaking Galileans? Then how is it that each of us hears them in his own native language? Parthians, Medes and Elamites; residents of Mesopotamia, Judea and Cappadocia, Pontus and Asia, Phrygia and Pamphylia, Egypt and the parts of Libya near Cyrene; visitors from Rome (both Jews and converts to Judaism); Cretans and Arabs—we hear them declaring the wonders of God in our own tongues!'"

No wonder the Bible records that 3000 men came to faith in Jesus as Messiah that day. I want to paint a picture for you as we examine the events of the day of Pentecost. We need to ask ourselves some basis questions surrounding the details of this event. How was it that there just happened to be all these thousands of men at the Temple that day? Was that a normal amount of activity for any given day, or was there something happening that day that perhaps we are just unaware of?

The Bible declares that there are three pilgrim Feasts in which all men must attend. They are Passover, Pentecost and Tabernacles (Deuteronomy 16:16). What that means is that all males had to go to Jerusalem for these commanded Feasts of the Lord. The implication is that making the journey to Jerusalem for the other Feasts was optional, but these three were mandatory. Therefore we can deduct that at this particular Feast of Pentecost, being one of the Pilgrim Feasts, all males living in and around Israel were at the Temple on that day to celebrate the Feast of Pentecost.

The text says that when the day of Pentecost was "fully come...".
What does that mean? God told the people that they were to count seven
weeks from the Feast of Firstfruits, and then on the 50th day they were to
celebrate Pentecost. This was known as the "Counting of the Omer". So
the Feasts had "fully come" on the 50th day. So now we know why all
those men were at the Temple, but why were these men who had—only
50 days before—rejected Jesus and now they are literally pleading with
Peter to tell them how they can come to faith in Jesus as Messiah?

Let's replay the events of that morning. We've established that
Pentecost was a pilgrim feast. Men from all over Israel and the surrounding area are there. They are in the Temple and they are worshipping the
Lord. They are thanking God for giving them the Torah. The Feast of
Pentecost is the celebration of the giving of the Law. The people were
expecting God to do something they had read about for generations. They
knew one day God would take the law from tablets of stone and write the
law in their hearts. They looked forward to this day for all of time.

Read what the prophet said in Jeremiah 31:31-33—*"'The time is coming,' declares the Lord, 'when I will make a new covenant with the house
of Israel and with the house of Judah. It will not be like the covenant I
made with their forefathers when I took them by the hand to lead them out
of Egypt, because they broke my covenant, though I was a husband to
them,' declares the Lord. 'This is the covenant I will make with the house
of Israel after that time,' declares the Lord. 'I will put my law in their
minds and write it on their hearts. I will be their God, and they will be my
people.'"*

The promise was that one day God would write His law in their hearts
by His Spirit. He no longer wanted a people who just knew the Law with
their minds. He did not want the Law to be written in stone any longer,
but rather He wanted it to be written in their hearts. During the Temple
service they would have read this passage. They would also have read
from the book of Joel—that's why Peter quotes from it when he address-
es the crowd. They were reminded of how God spoke to them through
thunder and fire and all kinds of marvelous signs. Imagine what must
have been happening in the minds of these men as they were leaving the
Temple area.

Remember what they had just read in the service. As they leave they
begin to hear the sound of a mighty rushing wind and of thunder. As they
are descending the Mount of Olives they see fire falling from the heavens
and they hear the voices through the fire in all types of different languages and dialects on that very day—the anniversary of the first time

something like this had happened in history. No wonder 3000 of them accepted Christ that day. There was no room for interpretation or error. The words of the prophets were coming to pass right in front of their eyes and they knew it.

By having an understanding of the culture and the Feasts, it can only enhance our understanding of the Biblical text. The day is coming to the Church when we will embrace the culture and the Feasts of the Lord. All over the world God is doing great things in His church. We must remember that He is coming back for one bride. As we all strive to achieve unity in the faith, I believe that we are yet to see God's greatest outpouring in the Earth. Just like the Feast of Pentecost was about harvesting the fields, so we to look forward to the great harvest of souls that God has promised to His people. This brings us to the conclusion of the Spring Feasts or the "Fulfilled" Feasts. All of these Feasts were fulfilled in Christ at His first coming, now we will look at the Fall Feasts and see how they point to events surrounding his second and glorious return!

THE FEAST OF TRUMPETS

Leviticus 23:23-25—*"The Lord said to Moses, 'Say to the Israelites: 'On the first day of the seventh month you are to have a day of rest, a sacred assembly commemorated with trumpet blasts. Do no regular work, but present an offering made to the Lord by fire.'"*

Deuteronomy 1:1—*"On the first day of the seventh month hold a sacred assembly and do no regular work. It is a day for you to sound the trumpets."*

Numbers 29:1—*"On the first day of the seventh month hold a sacred assembly and do no regular work. It is a day for you to sound the trumpets."*

This Feast takes place on the seventh month on the Jewish calendar known as Tishri, and it was on this day God told them to celebrate this Feast. The Feast of Trumpets is the one Feast in which the simplest commands were given in respects to its requirements. He said, "Blow Trumpets". Such a simple command from the Lord, but yet this Feast holds the greatest joy that a believer in Christ can hope for. This Feast is a prophetic picture or type of the Rapture of the Bride of Christ.

Trumpets have a very significant role in Scripture. It's important for us to pause for a few moments and dig up the nuggets of gold this Feast holds for us. Let's look at a couple of verses in Scripture that deal with the blowing of trumpets. The first one is found in Matthew 24:31—*"And he will send his angels with a loud trumpet call, and they will gather his elect from the four winds, from one end of the heavens to the other."* Another is found in Joel 2:1—*"Blow the trumpet in Zion; sound the alarm on my holy hill. Let all who live in the land tremble, for the day of the Lord is coming. It is close at hand..."*

The Feast of Trumpets is the name given to this Feast in Scripture. Most people today would know this Feast by its modern name of "Rosh Hashanah". It literally means, "Head of the year". Just like Passover begins the Jewish religious year, Trumpets begins the Jewish Civil year. So in the Jewish community Rosh Hashanah is celebrated as the New Year. There are different reasons for this. Rabbinical tradition teaches that the world was created on Tishri 1, and some even teach that this was the very day in which man was created. During Bible times this Feast was celebrated for only one day. However, as time went on, it was extended to be celebrated for an additional day.

The New Year is determined by the sighting of the new moon by two witnesses. To minimize the chance of an error in the sighting of the new moon and therefore celebrate the Feast on the wrong date they added one day just to be safe. The Feast of Trumpets is the only Feast in which no one really knows the day or hour in which it will begin. They always know the season of Trumpets but they can't pinpoint the day. It was to this event that Jesus referred to in His comments about the end times in Matthew 24:36—*"No one knows about that day or hour, not even the angels in heaven, nor the Son, but only the Father."*

It's interesting to note that it is necessary for two witnesses to come before the Feast of Trumpets can begin. In the book of Revelation, John mentions that two witnesses will be sent by God in the last days, it is very likely that these are the two witnesses that must come before the rapture can take place. Consider the text and then we will consider the author and his culture. Revelation 11:3-4—*"And I will give power to my two witnesses, and they will prophesy for 1,260 days, clothed in sackcloth. These are the two olive trees and the two lampstands that stand before the Lord of the earth."* You have to remember that John was a Jewish male living within First Century Israel. The fact that he received the revelation at Patmos has little or no relevance to his theology and influences. As a First Century Jew, the Judaism of the day would have been the religion for what his prophecies were based upon. The idea of two witnesses coming before Trumpets can begin is very much a First Century Jewish idea.

We are using the word trumpet quite a bit, but what do we mean when we say trumpet? Actually, the Hebrew word for trumpet in regards to the Feast is the word "Shofar". The shofar is a ram's horn and was used at all the sacred gatherings of Israel and to make various pronouncements in the land. The following are nine different purposes for the trumpet in Bible times. They were used for the calling of assemblies. They were blown at the journeying of the camps. They were sounded for the calling of princes and also for the blowing of alarms. They were blown in times of war or enemy oppression. They were used for days of gladness as well as for solemn assemblies. They were blown at the beginning of each month and they were also sounded during times of offerings and sacrifices. As you can see, trumpets played a major role in ancient Israel.

Trumpets were also used in the coronation ceremony of a new king. They were blown on the great day of the dedication of Solomon's temple and for the great year of jubilee. Trumpets also play an important role when it comes to end time events such as God's final judgment and, of course, in relation to the Rapture and Second Coming of Christ. This Feast takes place on the first day of the seventh month; actually all the prophetic Feasts take place in the seventh month. It's interesting that God should choose the seventh month for the end time Feasts to be celebrated. It is clear in Scripture that the number seven has a reoccurring role in God's end time plans. The number seven represent completion and rest; it's no coincidence that God should choose these dates.

Like all of Israel's Feasts, this Feast also had natural, as well as supernatural, implications surrounding it. Also, like so many of the other Feasts, Rosh Hashanah has its own traditions and prophetic significance. The Feast of Trumpets is a time of reflection and forgiveness. This Feast begins the season of what has come to be known as Israel's highest Holy Days of the year. The Feast of Trumpets is celebrated on the first day and then The Day of Atonement (or Yom Kippur) is celebrated on the tenth day where He will execute His judgment. It's believed that the time between trumpets and Atonement is when a person has the opportunity to seek forgiveness and for the Lord's wrath to pass over them. Literally, on the Day of Atonement God decides whether a person will live or die that year as well as whether they will be blessed or not. So those days between trumpets and Atonement are meant for making things right and for confession and restoration of relationships. Thus, those few days are the most important days on the Jewish calendar, both in Biblical and now in modern times.

According to Jewish tradition there are several things that happen during the Feast of Trumpets. The purpose of this work is not to repeat information that has already been put into print, but rather to bring fresh new insight into the meaning and purpose of the Feasts. We will however er mention a couple of the traditional beliefs about this holiday in order to help us better understand its prophetic implications. The first tradition held is that on the Day of Trumpets that three books are opened up in heaven by God: The book of life for the wicked, the book of life for the righteous, and the book of life for the in-between.

We stated earlier that trumpets marked the beginning of the high holy days and what has also been called the days of awe. God would open up His books in heaven and wait to make His judgment on the Day of Atonement. This might sound odd to us, but there are several Scriptures that talk about different books being opened and names being either written or removed from their pages. Let's look at a few verses both in the Old and the New Testament. Let us keep in mind that these are traditions associated with the Feasts and we are in no way implying them as truth but rather only present them to you so that you will have a better understanding of the background of this Feast. oly days also known as the great days of awe.

Psalms 69:28—*"May they be blotted out of the book of life and not be listed with the righteous."*

Exodus 32:32-33—*"But now, please forgive their sin—but if not, then blot me out of the book you have written.' The Lord replied to Moses, 'Whoever has sinned against me I will blot out of my book.'"*

Revelation 3:5—*"He who overcomes will, like them, be dressed in white. I will never blot out his name from the book of life, but will acknowledge his name before my Father and his angels."*

Revelation 20:12—*"And I saw the dead, great and small, standing before the throne, and books were opened. Another book was opened, which is the book of life. The dead were judged according to what they had done as recorded in the books."*

These are but a few references to help us understand the thinking behind some of these ideas. So because it is in this time period that God writes or blots out the name of people from His book, tradition also teaches that it was during this Feast that Satan would come to tempt and lead people away from God so that their names would not go into the book of life. Jewish tradition teaches the blast of the Shofar would confuse Satan and would therefore prevent Him from bringing accusation against the people of God. So it's no small wonder why today there are over one hundred blasts during the Rosh Hashanah ceremony.

Another tradition that is associated with this Feast is what is known as the "Casting Ceremony". During this ceremony you are to go down to a stream or river and empty all of your pockets of bread crumbs and leaven. You are to them throw the bread into the water. The bread is symbolic of sin and casting it into the water is symbolic of forgiveness. This ceremony has its roots in Micah 7:18-19—*"Who is a God like you, who pardons sin and forgives the transgression of the remnant of his inheritance? You do not stay angry forever but delight to show mercy. You will again have compassion on us; you will tread our sins underfoot and hurl all our iniquities into the depths of the sea."*

Another tradition of Rosh Hashanah is a rabbinical teaching regarding resurrection. Ancient Jewish theology teaches that the resurrection from the dead takes place on the first day of the Feast of Trumpets. The Scriptures are replete with references to trumpet sounds and their link to resurrection. This belief is not only ancient but modern as well. If you ever have a chance to walk through a Jewish cemetery you fill find the many of the grave stones have pictures of Shofar's engraved on top them reflecting the belief that the dearly departed one will be resurrected at the sound of the trumpet.

This theology is also carried over into the New Testament. In fact, the Apostle Paul makes reference to this on more than one occasion. Paul's Jewishness is clearly illustrated in his doctrine concerning the resurrection. We need to remember that although the apostle Paul was born in Tarsus, he was theologically trained in Jerusalem. He was well versed as a Pharisee and even mentions this in Acts 23:6—*"Then Paul, knowing that some of them were Sadducees and the others Pharisees, called out in the Sanhedrin, 'My brothers, I am a Pharisee, the son of a Pharisee. I stand on trial because of my hope in the resurrection of the dead.'"*

In recent days the church is coming to realize and embrace the Jewishness of Jesus more and more and are allowing that knowledge to affect the way they see Jesus and His teachings. I would suggest that it is also very important for Christians to consider Paul in the same manner. Paul was a Jew in every way and makes mention of this fact quite clearly in Scripture. We must understand Paul's view of theology from a Hebrew perspective. Yes, Paul was the apostle to the Gentiles, but never forget who and what he was. Philippians 3:3-6—*"For it is we who are the circumcision, we who worship by the Spirit of God, who glory in Christ Jesus, and who put no confidence in the flesh—though I myself have reasons for such confidence. If anyone else thinks he has reasons to put confidence in the flesh, I have more: circumcised on the eighth day, of the people of Israel, of the tribe of Benjamin, a Hebrew of Hebrews; in regard to the law, a Pharisee; as for zeal, persecuting the church; as for legalistic righteousness, faultless."*

Consider Paul's doctrine about the resurrection as he writes in 1 Corinthians 15:51-52—*"Listen, I tell you a mystery: We will not all sleep, but we will all be changed—in a flash, in the twinkling of an eye, at the last trumpet. For the trumpet will sound, the dead will be raised imperishable, and we will be changed."*

Again in 1 Thessalonians 4:16-18—*"Brothers, we do not want you to be ignorant about those who fall asleep, or to grieve like the rest of men, who have no hope. We believe that Jesus died and rose again and so we believe that God will bring with Jesus those who have fallen asleep in him. According to the Lord's own word, we tell you that we who are still alive, who are left till the coming of the Lord, will certainly not precede those who have fallen asleep. For the Lord himself will come down from heaven, with a loud command, with the voice of the archangel and with the trumpet call of God, and the dead in Christ will rise first. After that, we who are still alive and are left will be caught up together with them in the clouds to meet the Lord in the air. And so we will be with the Lord for-*

ever. Therefore encourage each other with these words." Paul's view of the resurrection is consistent with the Jewish perspective of resurrection.

The Feast of Trumpets is a beautiful prophetic picture of the Rapture of the Bride of Christ—the Church. Since Christianity's earliest roots, there has been much debate about the rapture. Some scholars doubt its very existence while others hold various views about it and the end times. There are three distinct views in direct relation to the rapture. They are Pre-Tribulation, Mid-Tribulation and Post-Tribulation.

Pre-Tribulation holds to the view that the Church will be raptured before the tribulation period begin. The Mid-Tribulation view states that the Church will be raptured half way into the tribulation. And Post-Tribulation holds that the Church will endure the entire Tribulation and then be raptured. It is not the purpose of this work to explore and examine these different views. What we will do is present to you some parallels between an ancient Jewish wedding feast and some of the response that Jesus Himself gave concerning the end times and allow you to come to your own decision.

The Bible speaks often of Jesus and His bride, and in several cases, we—the Church—are directly called the bride of Christ. Why that name for the Church? Do Jesus and Paul simply use this language because it sounds nice, or is there a real purpose behind it? As we begin to understand the ancient Jewish betrothal and wedding practices, then the Scriptures regarding the end times begin to become clear for us.

The people in Jesus' day knew exactly what He was going to do in the last days because they understood the principles of betrothal and marriage. It merits some exploration at least. Look at what Paul says in Ephesians 5:31-32—*"For this reason a man will leave his father and mother and be united to his wife, and the two will become one flesh. This is a profound mystery—but I am talking about Christ and the church."* It seems to be quite clear that Paul is directly linking the rituals of an ancient wedding ceremony to Christ and His Church. Let us now look at some of these practices. First we will see what the actual ancient act was and then we will see how Jesus fulfilled and may fulfill the requirements

The Marriage Covenant and the Bride Price

When it came time in ancient Israel for a man to marry he would have to first go to the woman's house to present not only her, but her father as well, with a marriage covenant. Basically this document clearly outlined to the girl and her father how it was that this young man was going to provide for her. He would state his occupation and salary, living arrangements and pretty much just his general plans and intentions for her. In today's society, a man just asks the father's blessing and permission to marry the daughter, but in ancient Israel it was a much more involved process.

The father and the bride would both make the decision to accept or reject the man's offer. In the midst of all the plans of the covenant, one of the most important things was the bride's price. How much was this young man willing to pay and do for this beautiful woman that he wanted to marry? Not only would the bride price help compensate the family, but, more importantly, it demonstrated to the father how much he loved his daughter. The higher the price, the deeper the demonstration of his love for the girl.

Keeping this first step of betrothal in mind, let's determine exactly how Jesus carried out this first step of the process. At His final Passover supper with His disciples he accomplished the first requirement. He clearly stated to all those were gathered there how He was establishing a new covenant with them. He would provide for this covenant with the breaking of His body and by shedding His blood to fulfill the requirements necessary to keep the covenant.

In respect to the bride price He stated that He would pay for it with His love. Remember that the amount of the bride price determined the level of love. How great was His love for us? Enough to give His life for us. So we clearly see how Jesus kept the first step in the process of betrothal.

1 Corinthians 6:19-20—*"Do you not know that your body is a temple of the Holy Spirit, who is in you, whom you have received from God? You are not your own; you were bought at a price. Therefore honor God with your body."*

1 Peter 1:18-19—*"For you know that it was not with perishable things such as silver or gold that you were redeemed from the empty way of life handed down to you from your forefathers, but with the precious blood of Christ, a lamb without blemish or defect."*

Knocking on the Door

When the price was met, the daughter was notified. She then would prepare a betrothal meal if she wanted to marry him. The man would knock on her door and wait. If she was ready, the woman would open the door just a crack, which meant yes. The man would then be welcome to open the door and walk in to sit with her and share the meal. They would feed each other and drink from the same cup.

In keeping with the traditions of the betrothal process, Christ too, comes to knock on the door of our hearts. One thing that's important for us to note is the potential bride had to open the door. The man would not walk into the room unless she opened it. In this example, we see we also need to open the door of our hearts and say yes to His covenant. We see this clearly illustrated in scripture when Jesus said, in Revelation 3:20— *"Here I am! I stand at the door and knock; if anyone hears my voice and opens the door, I will come in and eat with him, and he with me."*

The Cup

The next step of betrothal involved the pouring and drinking of a cup. After the man made his presentation to the girl she had to decide whether or not to accept his offer. After his presentation he would then pour a cup of wine and offer it to her. If she agreed to the terms of the covenant she would then take and drink the cup. This indicated that she had accepted his proposal.

Once she did this the couple was legally betrothed and could not get out of the marriage unless they got a paper of divorce. Another tradition was that the man also would take and drink the cup to indicate his joy that she had received the cup.

Betrothal was legally binding and was as valid as being married only without the consummation of the marriage. The couple would then separate and then begin to make their preparations for the wedding day. The couple would not see each other during this process. The betrothal period would usually last between twelve and eighteen months.

Just like the bridegroom poured and offered a cup of wine to his bride, Jesus also offered a cup of wine to His disciples in the upper room on the night of His final Passover meal. He offered the cup to each of them and told them to drink. The disciples were the foundation and the pillars that Jesus was going to use to build His Church. So their actions were on our behalf as well. Each one there that night received the cup and therefore was accepting the covenant He was offering to them. At that point the Church was betrothed to Christ.

Matthew 26:27-29—*"Then he took the cup, gave thanks and offered it to them, saying, 'Drink from it, all of you. This is my blood of the covenant, which is poured out for many for the forgiveness of sins. I tell you, I will not drink of this fruit of the vine from now on until that day when I drink it anew with you in my Father's kingdom.'"*

Gifts for the Bride

After the acceptance of the covenant the bridegroom would leave the woman with gifts. They were, first of all, to show his joy for her acceptance and also was a sign of affection for her. The gift was also to serve as a reminder of himself in his absence. He was about to go away for a long time, and so the gifts were a reminder to her of him. Every time she would use one of the gifts that he had left for her, it would remind her of him and bring a smile to her face. So the purpose of these gifts was to keep the bride focused on her groom in his absence.

Jesus also gave gifts to us, His bride. Several are listed in 1 Corinthians chapters 13 and 14. I think it's hugely important for us to remember the purpose of the gifts. Jesus left us the gifts for one very specific and important reason: to remind us of Him. Every time you exercise one of the gifts that you have been given, it should bring all the attention and the glory to Christ. Acts 2:38—*"Peter replied, 'Repent and be baptized, every one of you, in the name of Jesus Christ for the forgiveness of your sins. And you will receive the gift of the Holy Spirit.'"*

Preparing A Place

After the covenant had been established, they drank the cup, and he left the gifts, it was then time to depart for and go to prepare a place for his bride. The groom generally went back to his father's house to build a home for the woman. He would spend the next couple of years preparing this new dwelling place. It would be beautiful. After all, it was for the love of his life. Although the son would actually build the home, it was built according to the father's specifications.

This was the place where they would come to spend their first seven days together (their honeymoon), so it was also called the wedding chamber. Now the young man would not be able to go get his bride until the father had released him. So if he was asked when he was to go receive his bride, he would have to say he did not know the day, only his father knew when he could go to get his bride.

Jesus also had to leave His newly betrothed bride to begin the next step of preparation. Remember that the son would go back to his father's house to begin constructing the new home. Let's see what Jesus said about this in John 14:1-4—*"Do not let your hearts be troubled. Trust in God; trust also in me. In my Father's house are many rooms; if it were not so, I would have told you. I am going there to prepare a place for you. And if I go and prepare a place for you, I will come back and take you to be with me that you also may be where I am. You know the way to the place*

---

where I am going." It seems pretty clear to me that Jesus was making a direct parallel to the process of betrothal.

After the son went to his father's house and had built the home, remember that only the father could release the son to go get the bride. Again let us look at Scripture for confirmation. Look at the following two verses in respect to this step in that process. The first is found in Mark 13:32—*"No one knows about that day or hour, not even the angels in heaven, nor the Son, but only the Father."* The second is found in Acts 1:6-7—*"So when they met together, they asked him, 'Lord, are you at this time going to restore the kingdom to Israel?' He said to them: 'It is not for you to know the times or dates the Father has set by his own authority.'"* Again, it seems very clear that Jesus had the betrothal process in mind.

A Waiting Bride

While the groom was away preparing the wedding chamber, the bride had a responsibility as well. Her job was to be ready for his return. That's all she had to do. The covenant had been established and accepted, so all she had to do was to prepare herself for the day of his return. The bride was considered to be consecrated at this point. It was said of her that she had been bought with a price and was therefore set aside for the groom only. She would wear a veil over her head when she was out in public so that others knew she belonged only to her beloved. She would have saved all her money to use for her preparation period. She would not know the exact day or hour of his return, so she had to be ready at all times. Traditionally the groom would come at night and so she had to have her bags and lamps filled with oil ready by her bed side.

As the bride of Christ, we to are called to be consecrated or set apart for Him. Our task at this point is to prepare ourselves for His return. Sometimes the Church tends to get caught up in all sorts of things that cause quarrels and divisions amongst the brethren. We must never lose sight of our focus, which is to be prepared for when He comes. It's interesting how the woman would save her money for the wedding. This money that she would bring to the groom was called her dowry. Without it she would not be able to marry. Also the groom would give her money towards this dowry and she would not dare lose it. By keeping it safe and secure she showed her love for the groom.

That is why the woman who lost her coin rejoiced when she found it, because it was part of her dowry. We find parable of Jesus in Luke 15:8-9—*"Or suppose a woman has ten silver coins and loses one. Does she not light a lamp, sweep the house and search carefully until she finds it? And* when she finds it, she calls her friends and neighbors together and says, 'Rejoice with me; I have found my lost coin.'"

One can quickly see why Jesus told the parable of the ten virgins in context to his second coming. Matthew 25:1-13—"At that time the kingdom of heaven will be like ten virgins who took their lamps and went out to meet the bridegroom. Five of them were foolish and five were wise. The foolish ones took their lamps but did not take any oil with them. The wise, however, took oil in jars along with their lamps. The bridegroom was a long time in coming, and they all became drowsy and fell asleep. At midnight the cry rang out: 'Here's the bridegroom! Come out to meet him!'

"Then all the virgins woke up and trimmed their lamps. The foolish ones said to the wise, 'Give us some of your oil; our lamps are going out.' 'No,' they replied, 'there may not be enough for both us and you. Instead, go to those who sell oil and buy some for yourselves.' But while they were on their way to buy the oil, the bridegroom arrived. The virgins who were ready went in with him to the wedding banquet. And the door was shut. Later the others also came. 'Sir! Sir!' they said. 'Open the door for us!' But he replied, 'I tell you the truth, I don't know you.' Therefore keep watch, because you do not know the day or the hour." We want to make sure we are ready!

The Coming of the Groom

The day would finally arrive when the father would release the son to go get his bride. What an exciting day! Both the groom and the bride had been waiting with great anticipation and excitement for the hour to arrive. The groom and his groomsmen would go ahead of him to the gate of the city where the bride lived. He would then sound the Shofar to let her know that her groom had finally come. At the blast of the trumpet sound she would leave her home and come part of the way to the gate where the groom would be waiting for her. He would then take her away to the wedding chamber where they would spend the next seven days together. It's good for us to be reminded of the fact that the groom generally came to "steal his bride away" during the night. And so the phrase "he will come like a thief in the night" has its roots in this ancient Jewish wedding tradition.

Just like the groom would come in the middle of the night to steal his bride away at the shout of the Shofar, and meet her half way, so too will Christ come for us. As a First Century Jew, Paul states this so well and so clearly in 1 Thessalonians 5:16-17—"For the Lord himself will come down from heaven, with a loud command, with the voice of the archangel *and with the trumpet call of God, and the dead in Christ will rise first. After that, we who are still alive and are left will be caught up together with them in the clouds to meet the Lord in the air. And so we will be with the Lord forever."* I find it nearly impossible to believe that the apostle Paul did not have the betrothal and covenant ritual in mind when, by the Holy Spirit, he penned those words. Again, Paul makes reference to these betrothal practices in 1 Thessalonians 5:1-2—*"Now, brothers, about times and dates we do not need to write to you, for you know very well that the day of the Lord will come like a thief in the night."*

Seven Days in the Wedding Chamber

After he came to take his bride away, the groom would take her back to his father's house to what was called the wedding chamber. This is where we get our modern version of the honeymoon. They would spend the next seven days together on their own. Even the members of the wedding party would wait for the seven days to be over, then they would announce the consummation to all those who had gathered and then they would celebrate for the entire seven day period.

Ancient Jewish eschatology taught that there would be a seven year period "time of trouble" that would come upon the earth. It was also known as "Jacob's Trouble", or "The Birth Pains of the Messiah". It was believed that the righteous would be resurrected just before this time and that they would enter the wedding chamber with Messiah and be protected from this great and terrible time of trouble. Today, in Christian circles, this period of trouble is known to us as the "Great Tribulation."

If we continue to follow the logic of how Christ fulfilled all the other elements of the betrothal period, then it is with great confidence that we can accept that Christ will fulfill the prophetic elements and requirement of the marriage covenant. As the bride of Christ, we will be "caught up" before the time of trouble and will spend that seven year period in the wedding chamber in the Father's house. 1 Thessalonians 1:9-10—*"They tell how you turned to God from idols to serve the living and true God, and to wait for his Son from heaven, whom he raised from the dead—Jesus, who rescues us from the coming wrath."*

The Marriage Supper

After the seven days together in the wedding chamber they would then emerge together. They would participate in a most joyous feast with friends and family members. This was called the marriage supper and would officially bring the wedding celebration to a close.

Just like the bride and groom would celebrate together a great wedding feast, so Jesus and His bride will enter into a time of great rejoicing and celebration. Revelation 19:6-9—*"Then I heard what sounded like a great multitude, like the roar of rushing waters and like loud peals of thunder, shouting: 'Hallelujah! For our Lord God Almighty reigns. Let us rejoice and be glad and give him glory! For the wedding of the Lamb has come, and his bride has made herself ready. Fine linen, bright and clean, was given her to wear.' (Fine linen stands for the righteous acts of the saints.) Then the angel said to me, 'Write: 'Blessed are those who are invited to the wedding supper of the Lamb'!' And he added, 'These are the true words of God.'"*

Depart for Their New Home

After the marriage supper, the bride and the groom would depart for their new home that the groom had prepared for them. Even to this day, if you go to Israel you will see beautifully built houses with unfinished exposed rooms in the house, usually on the second floor or on an adjoining part of the property. If you ask the father of the home why he has these unfinished rooms, he will tell you that they are for his sons. So that when they get married, they will have a place to come back to and build a wedding chamber for his bride.

Just as the bride and bridegroom would emerge and return to their new home, so too will we return with Christ to our new home that He has prepared for us. Revelation 21:1-10—*"Then I saw a new heaven and a new earth, for the first heaven and the first earth had passed away, and there was no longer any sea. I saw the Holy City, the new Jerusalem, coming down out of heaven from God, prepared as a bride beautifully dressed for her husband. And I heard a loud voice from the throne saying, 'Now the dwelling of God is with men, and he will live with them. They will be his people, and God himself will be with them and be their God. He will wipe every tear from their eyes. There will be no more death or mourning or crying or pain, for the old order of things has passed away.' He who was seated on the throne said, 'I am making everything new!' Then he said, 'Write this down, for these words are trustworthy and true.' He said to me: 'It is done. I am the Alpha and the Omega, the Beginning and the End. To him who is thirsty I will give to drink without cost from the spring of the water of life. He who overcomes will inherit all this, and I will be his God and he will be my son. But the cowardly, the unbelieving, the vile, the murderers, the sexually immoral, those who practice magic arts, the idolaters and all liars—their place will be in the fiery lake of burning sulfur. This is the second death.' One of the seven angels who had the seven bowls full of the seven last plagues came and said to me, 'Come, I will show you the bride, the wife of the Lamb.' And he carried me away in the Spirit to a mountain great and high, and showed me the Holy City, Jerusalem, coming down out of heaven from God.'"*

Conclusion

We can see from the pattern of this ancient betrothal and wedding practice that Jesus did very much have them on His mind as he told the people about the events surrounding the last days and His second coming. In order for us to better understand Jesus, we must understand His culture and the practice of His day. Only when we begin to view Him and His words and actions from their proper context, will we have a new and clear insight into His teachings. May we all be ready for the great Trumpet sound of the Lord.

THE DAY OF ATONEMENT

Leviticus 16:29-34—*"'This is to be a lasting ordinance for you: On the tenth day of the seventh month you must deny yourselves and not do any work—whether native-born or an alien living among you—because on this day atonement will be made for you, to cleanse you. Then, before the Lord, you will be clean from all your sins. It is a Sabbath of rest, and you must deny yourselves; it is a lasting ordinance. The priest who is anointed and ordained to succeed his father as high priest is to make atonement. He is to put on the sacred linen garments and make atonement for the Most Holy Place, for the Tent of Meeting and the altar, and for the priests and all the people of the community. This is to be a lasting ordinance for you: Atonement is to be made once a year for all the sins of the Israelites.' And it was done, as the Lord commanded Moses."*

Leviticus 23:27-32—*"The tenth day of this seventh month is the Day of Atonement. Hold a sacred assembly and deny yourselves, and present an offering made to the Lord by fire. Do no work on that day, because it is the Day of Atonement, when atonement is made for you before the Lord your God. Anyone who does not deny himself on that day must be cut off from his people. I will destroy from among his people anyone who does any work on that day. You shall do no work at all. This is to be a lasting ordinance for the generations to come, wherever you live. It is a Sabbath of rest for you, and you must deny yourselves. From the evening of the ninth day of the month until the following evening you are to observe your Sabbath."*

The Day of Atonement takes place on Tishri 10 and it was—and still is—Israel's most holy day. We saw how the Feast of Trumpets was a picture of the rapture of the Church. The Day of Atonement is also filled with prophetic imagery. In the chapter that dealt with the Feast of Firstfruits we identified the Messianic role of the High Priest. We also see Messianic implications during this Feast as well. We stated that whenever we read about the duties of a Prophet, Priest or King, that they are Messianic types for us to identify because they reveal to us the actions and duties of Christ as well. The Day of Atonement speaks of the judgment of God. In modern Judaism, this is the day when God makes His decisions that will affect your life for the upcoming year. During Trumpets, the message was all about forgiveness and repentance. During Atonement, the message is judgment. While all the other holidays are feasts, the Day of Atonement is actually a fast. Because of the magnitude of the message of this holiday, it stands alone above all the rest.

This Biblical holiday is also known as "Yom Kippur". Yom Kippur translated into English simply means, "The Day of Atonement". This is the sixth holiday on God's prophetic calendar and it takes place during the seventh month. It's important to note at this time that all of the fall feasts take place during this month. We must remember that the number seven represents completion and/or perfection. So with this in mind, we can see why God chose this month for these feasts to occur because they complete God's plan for mankind.

While we've already discussed how important this day was for the people, we also need to remember what an important day is was for the High Priest of Israel. While the entire nation awaited God's decision for the future, the High Priest was preparing himself for the most important day of the year. This was the only day he was allowed to enter the Holy of Holies. On no other day could he come face to face with God's presence. If he was to enter the Holy of Holies at any other time, he would surely die. Yet, on this incredible day, he could and would come into the presence of Almighty God and offer sacrifices on behalf of the people for the atoning of their sins.

It's also good to mention at this point that the sacrifices offered on this day had to be repeated on an annual basis. They waited for the day when God would send His Lamb to not only atone for their sins, which was simply a covering up of their sins, but the Lamb would remove the stain of sin for all of time. After the High Priest made all of the required sacrifices for the Feast of Trumpets, he was to go into seclusion for seven days to avoid becoming defiled for his duties on the Day of Atonement.

Let's examine the Messianic implications of the duties of the High Priest. The Feast of Trumpets took place on Tishri 1 and was celebrated for two days. The Day of the Atonement was celebrated on the tenth day. That leaves us seven days between the two feasts. I do not believe that this is a mere coincidence, but a very purposeful intent by God. If Jesus is our High Priest, then He will keep and fulfill the expectations that were upon the High Priest. Just as the High Priest would go away for seven days after the Feast of Trumpets—which was a picture of the rapture—and then return on the Day of Atonement, Christ also will take His Bride away for seven years and return with her on the Day of Atonement.

To avoid speculation, we need to have scripture as the foundation for this reasoning. There was a sacrifice performed on this day that sets it apart from every other feast. During all other feasts, the animals were always sacrificed *on the altar*, but during this feast the High Priest would sacrifice a bull *between the porch and the altar* (this sacrifice was for the priests and their families). Having this area in mind, let's examine what it says in Joel 2:15-17—*"Blow the trumpet in Zion, declare a holy fast, call a sacred assembly. Gather the people, consecrate the assembly; bring together the elders, gather the children, those nursing at the breast. Let the bridegroom leave his room and the bride her chamber. Let the priests, who minister before the Lord, weep* **between the temple porch and the altar***. Let them say, 'Spare your people, O Lord. Do not make your inheritance an object of scorn, a byword among the nations. Why should they say among the peoples, 'Where is their God?'"*

The above mentioned text is the most solid proof that Jesus will return with His Bride on the Day of Atonement. Let's break down the verse a little bit to give further verification to this fact. The first verse says that a Shofar is to be sounded—this is in reference to the Feast of Trumpets. And then the prophet says that a fast is to be declared—we already mentioned that the Day of Atonement is the only Biblical holiday that is a fast. So because of this fact, we know that the prophet is referring to this particular feast.

Verse sixteen speaks of the Bridegroom leaving His room and the bride her chamber. This is most interesting language used by Joel. In the last chapter we discussed in great detail, the process of the betrothal requirements. We discussed how after the covenant had been established, the bride and groom would go away for seven days to their wedding chamber. Only after those seven days had passed would they be able to emerge together and be seen by all.

Look carefully at what this passage says—it says that after the sound of the trumpet the Groom would leave His chamber. The Hebrew word for chamber is "chedar". Joel then says the bride would leave her room. The Hebrew word used here is the word "chuppa" and this also means chamber. So obviously the bridge and groom have just come from the same place.

It then says at the appearance of the bride and Groom, they will find the ministers weeping between the porch and the altar. We already know that the Day of Atonement is the only feast on which the High Priest performed his duty between the porch and the altar. So, because of this fact, we know that this text is referring to the events that will take place during Yom Kippur. Because of the manner in which these duties were specified to be performed, we know that Christ and His bride will emerge for all to be seen during the great Day of Atonement.

Why is it when the bride and Groom return, the priests and people are weeping and crying out for God to spare them? It's because this event will take place at the end of the tribulation period and either those who were left behind or saved after the rapture will be crying out to God to escape tribulation.

The next sacrifice was for the people of Israel. There was a ceremony that involved two goats. The goats were brought in before the High Priest and lots were cast to decide the order of the sacrifice of each goat. The golden lots had inscriptions on them—one said "For Adonai" and the other was marked "For Azazel". There have been different interpretations for the meaning of "Azazel", but it's commonly agreed that it was a reference for Satan. The goat to which the lot of Adonai fell on was immediately sacrificed on the behalf of the people. The goat to which the lot of Azazel fell on was marked with a scarlet strip of wool that was tied around its horns.

At this point the High Priest would place his hands upon the head of the goat marked for Azazel and symbolically transfer the sins of the people to the goat. Following this practice, the goat was then released into the wilderness, thus carrying away the sins of the people. This ancient practice gives us our modern day term, "scapegoat". It's interesting that the goat was released into the desert and not into any other place. In ancient Israel, it was believed by the people that the desert was inhabited by demons and even Satan himself. Isn't it interesting that Jesus went into the desert to be tempted by Satan after His baptism by John? Consider what is found in Isaiah 13:20-22 (AMP)—*"Babylon shall never be inhabited or dwelt in from generation to generation; neither shall the Arab pitch his tent there, nor shall the shepherds make their sheepfolds there. But wild beasts of the desert will lie down there, and the people's houses will be full of dolefully howling creatures; and ostriches will dwell there, and wild goats [like demons] will dance there. And wolves and howling creatures will cry and answer in the deserted castles, and jackals in the pleasant palaces. And Babylon's time has nearly come, and her days will not be prolonged."*

Initially the goat was released into the desert. This practice was later revised because occasionally the goat would wander into a neighbouring town or city. In order to prevent this from happening, the rabbis introduced another practice into the Yom Kippur tradition. Instead of releasing the goat into the desert, the goat was actually brought to the edge of a cliff and thrown off the cliff backwards to ensure the act was complete. Before the priest would push the goat backwards, he would tear off a portion of the scarlet strip of wool that was tied around one of its horns. Ancient Jewish literature records a most phenomenal event—the piece of scarlet wool that the priest held in his hand would turn white as the goat fell. This was a sign to the people that their sins had in fact been forgiven and removed for another year. Consider what is written in Isaiah 1:18—*"'Come now, let us reason together,' says the Lord. 'Though your sins are like scarlet, they shall be as white as snow; though they are red as crimson, they shall be like wool.'"*

In the action of throwing the goat off the cliff, we see another Messianic role being fulfilled here. We also know that Christ will come and defeat the enemy as found in Revelations 20:10—*"And the devil, who deceived them, was thrown into the lake of burning sulfur, where the beast and the false prophet had been thrown. They will be tormented day and night for ever and ever."*

This practice was carried on for hundreds of years by the priests and brought great comfort and solace to the people. They knew every year that God would forgive their sins. Every year, as the scarlet wool turned white, they would take comfort in knowing that as long as the priest performed his duty in this manner, they would always have a means for the removal of sins. Ancient Jewish literature records that the scarlet piece of wool stopped turning white after the death and resurrection of Jesus. Can we consider this coincidence or divine design?

We know now that it is not by the blood of goats that we have forgiveness of sins because Christ—who is God's Passover Lamb—has been slain for us. In ancient days, the blood of goats only covered the sins of the people and had to be repeated year after year, but Christ died once for all. The Bible speaks clearly about this in Hebrews 10:1-14—*"The law is only a shadow of the good things that are coming—not the realities themselves. For this reason it can never, by the same sacrifices repeated endlessly year after year, make perfect those who draw near to worship. If it could, would they not have stopped being offered? For the worshipers would have been cleansed once for all, and would no longer have felt guilty for their sins. But those sacrifices are an annual reminder of sins, because it is impossible for the blood of bulls and goats to take away sins. Therefore, when Christ came into the world, he said: 'Sacrifice and offering you did not desire, but a body you prepared for me; with burnt offerings and sin offerings you were not pleased.' Then I said, 'Here I am—it is written about me in the scroll—I have come to do your will, O God.' First he said, 'Sacrifices and offerings, burnt offerings and sin offerings you did not desire, nor were you pleased with them' (although the law required them to be made). Then he said, 'Here I am, I have come to do your will.' He sets aside the first to establish the second. And by that will, we have been made holy through the sacrifice of the body of Jesus Christ once for all. Day after day every priest stands and performs his religious duties; again and again he offers the same sacrifices, which can never take away sins. But when this priest had offered for all time one sacrifice for sins, he sat down at the right hand of God. Since that time he waits for his enemies to be made his footstool, because by one sacrifice he has made perfect forever those who are being made holy."*

THE FEAST OF TABERNACLES

Leviticus 23:34—*"Say to the Israelites: 'On the fifteenth day of the seventh month the Lord's Feast of Tabernacles begins, and it lasts for seven days.'"*

Deuteronomy 16:13-16—*"Celebrate the Feast of Tabernacles for seven days after you have gathered the produce of your threshing floor and your winepress. Be joyful at your Feast—you, your sons and daughters, your menservants and maidservants, and the Levites, the aliens, the fatherless and the widows who live in your towns. For seven days celebrate the Feast to the Lord your God at the place the Lord will choose. For the Lord your God will bless you in all your harvest and in all the work of your hands, and your joy will be complete. Three times a year all your men must appear before the Lord your God at the place he will choose: at the Feast of Unleavened Bread, the Feast of Weeks and the Feast of Tabernacles. No man should appear before the Lord empty-handed."*

The Feast of Tabernacles takes place on the fifteenth day of the seventh month and is an annual reminder of Israel's forty year wandering in the desert. There are various names by which this feast is called. Its most common name is the one that we've already used which is the Feast of Tabernacles. It is also referred to as the Feast of Booths and by its Hebrew name—Sukkot. There are three basic aspects to this feast—it speaks to us in terms of God's past, present and future activity within mankind.

The Feast of Tabernacles reminds us of God's supernatural intervention during the freeing of the Israelites from Egyptian bondage. We are reminded of God's display of power as He led them through the Red Sea. We see how He provided for their every need as He took them from the shores of the land of slavery into the Promised Land. Every year we're reminded of how God rained down manna each day and how He caused water to come out of a rock to quench the thirst of an entire nation. The Feast of Tabernacles also reminds us of God's ever present nature. We remember how God directed them with a cloud by day and with a pillar of fire by night. The people dwelt in temporary dwellings called "sukkots". For forty years, God faithfully protected and provided for His children.

Today the Feast of Tabernacles falls during the time of the final harvest in Israel and it occurs just before their rainy season. It's a season of thanksgiving and rejoicing because of God's provision of the crops that year. God commanded that the people were to dwell in tabernacles for seven days. It's a time to separate ourselves from the comforts of life in order for us to identify with what the Israelites endured. As we live in the tabernacles, we are brought to a level of simplicity that helps free us from our slavery to materialism. As we dwell in the tabernacles, we are reminded of the fact that God is the source of our joy, and not our possessions. We remember that there is protection and safety in the covering of our God. We know that because He has provided, He will continue to provide.

Not only does the Feast of Tabernacles speak of God's activity in the past and in the present, but it also speaks of a time when God will once again intervene with humanity. We look forward with great anticipation to the day when, once again, God will "tabernacle" with man. As it was in the beginning, so shall it be in the end. A beautiful picture is painted for us about our glorious future in Revelation 21:1-3—*"Then I saw a new heaven and a new earth, for the first heaven and the first earth had passed away, and there was no longer any sea. I saw the Holy City, the New Jerusalem, coming down out of heaven from God, prepared as a bride beautifully dressed for her husband. And I heard a loud voice from the throne saying, 'Now the dwelling of God is with men, and he will live with them. They will be his people, and God himself will be with them and be their God.'"*

There are three distinct areas in relation to this feast that we want to deal with in this chapter. The first area is in regards to a tradition that evolved during the First Temple period which was the time of Solomon's Temple. King Solomon dedicated the Temple to the Lord during the Feast of Tabernacles. The Bible records an extraordinary event that took place during the dedication.

After Solomon prayed and dedicated the Temple, the Shekinah glory of God fell from heaven and filled the Temple. The fire actually lit the altar and the candles within the Holy of Holies. Because of this event, the people associated the Feast of Tabernacles with the return of the glory of God to the Temple—2 Chronicles 7:1-3—*"When Solomon finished praying, fire came down from heaven and consumed the burnt offering and the sacrifices, and the glory of the Lord filled the temple. The priests could not enter the temple of the Lord because the glory of the Lord filled it. When all the Israelites saw the fire coming down and the glory of the Lord above the temple, they knelt on the pavement with their faces to the ground, and they worshiped and gave thanks to the Lord, saying, 'He is good; his love endures forever.'"*

The Feast of Tabernacles

In the light of this association, between the Feast of Tabernacles and the return of the glory of God to the Temple, the accounts of the Gospel of John take on a new a powerful light. Before we read the scripture, let's go over in our minds what people were expecting during this feast. The glory of God filled the Temple on the last and greatest day of the Feast of Tabernacles. So, year after year, people anticipated the return of God's glory to the Temple on this very specific day.

The disciple John records for us in his gospel, the activity of Jesus during this feast time. It's important for us to remember that John was a First Century Jew writing to First Century Jews who knew and expected certain things to happen. On what day does John record for us that Jesus came into the Temple on? We have to remember to pay attention to the details of scripture. Events and details have not been placed there by chance; they are placed there because John wants to take his readers to a revelational discovery. This is what he writes in John 7:37—*"On the last and greatest day of the Feast, Jesus stood and said in a loud voice, 'If anyone is thirsty, let him come to me and drink.'"*

On what day does John record that Jesus came to the Temple? It was the last and greatest day of the Feast of Tabernacles. Why is this important?—because the people expected the glory of God to manifest itself in the Temple on that specific day. Simply, by Jesus presence in the Temple that day, it was one of His greatest Messianic claims. Jesus coming to the Temple on that specific day was God's way of saying to the people that here was the actual Glory of God that had returned to the Temple.

Another tradition associated with the Feast of Tabernacles is what is called the water libation ceremony. It was a visual prayer for rain. Israel did and does depend on the fall rains in order for a harvest to be reaped. Rain has always been a symbol of life to the Jewish people. During this ceremony, several steps were taken in order to ensure that God would once again send the rains that the land so desperately needed. The High Priest would exit the Temple and begin to descend down the side of the Mount of Olives and make his way down to the Pool of Siloam which was filled with living water (water that is spring fed and constantly moving). The High Priest would carry two golden pitchers with him and when he arrived at the pool, he would then dip and fill both pitchers with the living water. The procession would then leave the pool and make their journey back to the Temple area. Once the High Priest reached the altar, he would then begin to pour the living water over the altar. This ceremony was symbolically conducted and was done on each and every day of the feast. It was a prayer for God to send the living water and on the last day it would release faith in the people to believe that God would send them His living water that day.

Picture in your mind this water libation ceremony taking place and the following verse in John 7:37-38 where Jesus made a Messianic claim. It says: *"On the last and greatest day of the Feast, Jesus stood and said in a loud voice, 'If anyone is thirsty, let him come to me and drink. Whoever believes in me, as the Scripture has said, streams of living water will flow from within him.'"* By saying this, Jesus was implying that He was the Living Water sent from God that they were praying for. By knowing the events that were taking place in the background when Jesus made that statement, we see that it adds greater depth and understanding to the text.

There was another ceremony during the Feast of Tabernacles called the "Illumination of the Temple" Ceremony. Ancient Jewish literature records for us another practice that developed over time which was in operation during the time Christ walked the earth. There were four large menorahs in the temple courtyard. Some literature suggests that these menorahs were a staggering 70 feet tall. In any event we know that they were very large in size. During each day of the feast, these menorahs were lit in an area of the Temple known as the Women's Court. They were lit every day and it was said of them that they cast such a bright light that every courtyard in Jerusalem was lit because of them. Once again, with this ceremony in the forefront of our minds, we come to the statement of Jesus in John 8:12—*"When Jesus spoke again to the people, he said, 'I am the light of the world. Whoever follows me will never walk in darkness, but will have the light of life.'"* When He made this statement, both the people and the priests knew exactly what Jesus was referring to. For six nights they saw the blazing light of the fire in the Temple courts, so in this context the words of Jesus are powerful.

Shortly after leaving the temple, Jesus reinforces His statements—as He often did—with actions. He did not just claim to be the Light of the World; he powerfully displayed to them that He was, in fact, what and who He said He was. After he had made the claim, *"I am the light of the world,"* in the Temple courts, he went on to prove it by healing a man who was born blind as found in John 9:1-7—*"As he went along, he saw a man blind from birth. His disciples asked him, 'Rabbi, who sinned, this man or his parents, that he was born blind?' 'Neither this man nor his parents sinned,' said Jesus, 'but this happened so that the work of God might be displayed in his life. As long as it is day, we must do the work of him who sent me. Night is coming, when no one can work. While I am in the world,*

I am the light of the world.' Having said this, he spit on the ground, made some mud with the saliva, and put it on the man's eyes. 'Go,' he told him, 'wash in the Pool of Siloam' (this word means Sent). So the man went and washed, and came home seeing."

The most powerful message of the Feast of Tabernacles is the fact of God's desire to have intimate fellowship with His creation. Since sin first entered the world, it has been God's desire to have the relationship reconciled. We know that Christ has reconciled man unto God and in and through His birth, life and death, God has made His dwelling with man. Not only was Jesus the Tabernacle of God, but He also came to tabernacle with man as found in John 1:14 (AMP)—*"And the Word (Christ) became flesh (human, incarnate) and tabernacled (fixed His tent of flesh, lived awhile) among us; and we [actually] saw His glory (His honor, His majesty), such glory as an only begotten son receives from his father, full of grace (favour, loving-kindness) and truth."*

To order additional copies of

FIRST CENTURY FOUNDATIONS

Please Write:
Operation Outreach
908 Lancaster Blvd.
Milton, ON L9T 6A4
Canada

Phone:
(905) 876-2557

Fax:
(905) 875-9878

E-mail:
joe@operationoutreach.ca

To view other resources on our website, please visit
www.operationoutreach.ca